This book is dedicated to Alan Card,
with thanks to Cameron Spencer and
Denise Michell.

Pegasus Flies

Poems and Musings

rosie temple

Publishing rosietempleart
Illustrations rosie temple

www.rosietempleart.com
© 2020 rosietemple. All Rights Reserved.
ISBN: 9798580589923

Table of contents:

Chapter One

The Avalonians

New Avalonians,
Actual Avalonians,
Old Avalonians,
Future Avalonians,
Living Avalonians,
Long Dead Ghostly Avalonians,
Anaemic Vegan Avalonians,
Silly Sausage Avalonians,
Still Sometimes Stupid Avalonians,
Dyslexic Avalonians who can't spell Avalions,
Free Thinking but Stinky Avalonians,
Funny Hunny Eating Avalonians,
Tricky, Sticky Avalonians,
Wild, Woolly, Horny Avalonians,
Glam and Goddessey Avalonians
Dog-on-String Walking Avalonians,
Grumpy, Lumpy Avalonians,
Sleepy, Weepy Avalonians,
Star Gazy Pie Making Avalonians,
Sing Although Your Heart is Breaking
Avalonians,
Hopi Dopey Avalonians,

Leather Jacketed and Shaded Esoteric
Avalonians,
Orange Trousered Ley Line Hunting
Avalonians,
Very Very Stinking Rich Hiding Avalonians,
Fancy Jacketed Astrology Touting Avalonians,
Grungy, Sexy Avalonians,
Spooky Tor Tunnelling Avalonians,
New Avant Garde Arty Avalonians,
Secretive, Silent Avalonians,
Ugly, Happy Clappy Avalonians,
Purple Velvet Clad Large American
Avalonians,
Yak Milk Skinny Latte Drinking Avalonians,
Green Haired Witchy Bitchy Avalonians,
Graceful Ballerina Avaloninas.
Avalon: She belongs to us all and to none of
us too.

If you live in Avalon,
And maybe you do?

You are an Avalonian,
Plain and Simple
And you are ENOUGH.

If you don't, then you don't!

Forging Diamond Consciousness

You Strangled me at John O'Groats
You Sent me Round the Bend
You put Lapis Lazuli at my Throat
And Loved me Badly at Lands' End

We Danced in Firelight On Aquamarine
Shores
You gave me Tons of Adventurine
We Idled in Dorset's Old Bridleways
And on Hyde Park's Serpentine

You Led me to the Higher Heart
With Roses and Pink Tormaline
You Gave me Blood Red Rubies
And the Biggest Opal I have Seen

We Never Climbed up Glastonbury Tor
But We Might Yet some Misty Morn
We did Find the Rarest Selenite
And Eschewed the Rhino Horn

On the Tor when the Phoenix had Flown
We Found the Tablets of Emerald Green
You Placed the Sunstone on my Heart
In that Holy Timeless Scene

We Gambolled and Giggled Like Lambkins
In Palaces of Jasper and Jade
We Drummed out our Hearts in the Darkness
While Gypsy Musicians Played

You Dived Down to the Darkest Depths
And Became the Maddest Clown
You Blew a Star up for the Gold
You Placed upon my Crown

From Obsidian Plutonic Depths
From Drudgery and Hard Grind
From Scholastic Monastic Midnight Oil
You Forged my Diamond Mind

Equinox

When Hopes and Dreams
And Old Fantasies,
And Phantoms of Delight,
Who saw you through many
A Summer's Lonely, Empty Night,
All have to Die
In Autumn Bonfires,
And Vanity and all her Sisters,
Scream Wildly
Through Throat Constricting Smoke,
That they do not wish to Die.

When Last Year's
Half Hearted Promises
Fade and Rot in the Ground
With the Autumn Leaves
To be Mulch for
Tomorrow's Prized Tomatoes;
The Scarlett Cherries of
Yesterday's Frozen Tears,
Whose buried Fears and Sorrows
Must be left where they Lie.

When Libra's Honest Scales
Weigh your Heart once again
Against a White Feather,

And the Gentle Rain Reminds you
That the Dove of Peace is coming,
With her Holy Branch.
She will deliver it softly, softly,
In your meditation,
Unnoticed by the World.

Then Kiss your Dreams of Love
Goodbye,
And Go Outside
And Kiss the Sky

Glastonbury Poem

A WORK IN PROGRESS. PLEASE ADD TO IT......

Spacey, Flakey,
Dope Cake Makey,
Hippy, Trippy,
Hummus Dippy,
Sandal Wearing,
Caring, Sharing,
Muesli Munching,
Cliquey Bunching,
Tor Climbings,
Book Signings,
Morals Flinging,
Crystals Singing,
Grail Seekers,
Chick Pea Tikkas,
Future Seers,
Fake Piers,
Flipping Poles,
Rabbit Holes,
Dreadlock Sporting,

Bad Things Snorting,
Weed Potting,
Goddess Spotting,
Egyp-tian Pyra-mids,
Vesica Pisces Well Lids,
Taurus Fields,
Psychic Shields,
Ashram Chanting,
Thorn Tree Planting,
Arthur's Seating,
Prasad Eating,
World Beating,
Eco Heating,
Ale Flagons,
Dancing Dragons,
Walk Ins,
Drop Outs,
Late Night
Drunken Shouts,
Bawdy Bards,
Tarot Cards,
Round Table,
Just a Fable?
Moon Barking,
Sky Larking,
Ley Line Hunting,
Mrs Bunting,

Gypsy Singers,
Phantom Flingers,
Holding Space,
In your Face,
Music Streaming,
Yoni Steaming,
Fire Walking,
Facebook Stalking,
Cannabis Toking,
Incense Smoking,
White Spring
Red Spring
Matrix Hacks,
Zodiacs,
Short Skirts,
Bad Flirts,
Tall Hats,
Yoga Mats,
Green Hair,
Cassie's Chair,
Tantric Sex,
Bouncing Cheques,
Pukka Pies,
Honeyed Lies,
Hot Tubs,
Snidey Snubs,
Star Gates,

Mates Rates,
Planets Working
Out Fates,
Moon Lodges,
Tax Dodges,
Lake Ladies,
Life In Hades,
Green Men,
Oh Why?
Oh When?
Michael Eavis,
Butthead's Beavis,
Vegan Cheesey,
Pilgrim Pleasey,
Abbey Monks,
Ganesh Trunks,
Void Moons,
Looney Tunes,
Bleeding Hearts,
Astro Charts,
Urban Monks,
Rarely Hunks,
Steam Punks,
Tofu Chunks,
Plant Based
Potlucking,
Eco Friendly

Cars and Trucking,
Sofa Surfing,
Astro Turfing,
Bed Hopping,
Charity Shopping,
Ley Lines,
Maltwood Signs,
Rebels,
Activists,
Late Nights,
Drunken Fists,
Conspiracy Theory,
Oh So Dreary,
Conspiracy Fact,
Rarely Backed,
Dogs on Strings,
Fairy Wings,
Oh Look!
There's a Druid,
Quaffing Dodgy
Apple Fluid,
Homelessness,
Restlessness,
Heart Callings,
Heart Fallings,
Heart Breakings,
No Takings,

Cheap Seats,
Cheap Suits,
Free Lunches,
Witchy Hunches,
Buskers Plucking,
Doobie Sucking,
Lion's Gate,
Love and Hate,
Full Moons,
Lover's Spoons,
Handfasting,
Is it Lasting?
Holy Grail,
Will you Fail?
Will the No
Come in the Mail?
Gas Lighting,
Moonlighting,
Bible Bashings,
Tongue Lashings,
Try Out Initiations,
Dodgy Recalibrations,
Past Life Readings,
Group Misleadings,
Healy Feely,
Really? Really?
Crop Circles,

Mrs Burcles,
Pixie Balls,
Fairy Halls,
Goddesses Bouncing
Off the Walls,
Temples Whirling,
Lies Unfurling,
Good Crack,
Good Cheer,
Lancelot, Guinevere,
Lance of Light,
Naughty Knight?
Pole Star, Old Star,
New Star, Ishtar,
Are you Sirius?
Wimble Toot,
Beetlejuice,
Maltwood moot
Butt Close,
Leg Of Mutton,
Wagg Drove,
Johnny Button,
New Age -
Old Age,
Weirdos Seeking
Jimmy Paige,

Time Line Jumping,
Twin Flame Humping,
Kind Hearts,
Coronets,
Bookies Taking,
Fred's Bets........
Mad Hats,
Total Twats,
Loud Drumming,
Sexy Strumming,
Smoke and Feathers,
Misty Weathers,
Sunsets, Resets,
Lettings and Unholy Bets
Solstice, Equinox,
Alice and Goldilocks,
Night Star Gazing,
Phoenix Blazing,
Michael Line,
Mary Line,
Abbey Grounds
In Hot Sunshine,
Fairy's Holding Hands,
Declaring
Their Marriage Bans,
Ooooohhhhh
There Goes Nicholas Cage,

Bringing in the Aquarian Age,
Pricey Organic Wines,
Morrison's Car Parking Fines,
Frost Fayre,
Lady Mayor,
Or-ganic Farming,
Bards A-Charming,
Wiggly Sticks,
No Stevie Nicks, (AAAH!)
Uploading,
Downloading,
Meditation,
Freeloading,
Hundred Monkeys,
Winking Turtle,
Rainbows End,
The Duck at Burtle,
Goth Vicars,
No Knickers,
Witches Hats,
Black Cats,
Dealers Wheeling,
Healers Healing,
Lovers Meeting,
Lots of Tweeting.........

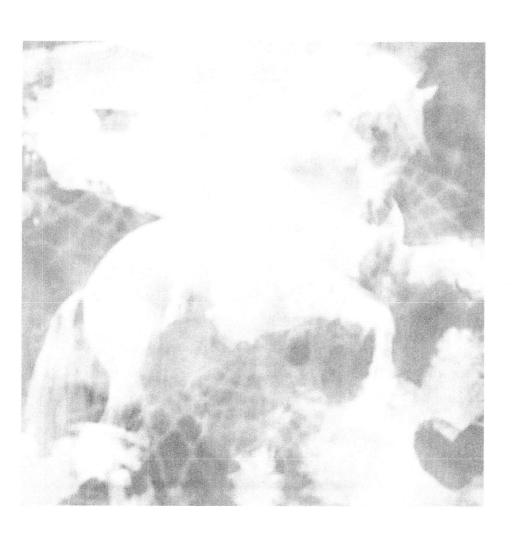

Restart the World; I want to Stay On It

They can stop the World, it Seems,
But You still can't Get Off.
They can Stop the Economy
But You Can't Eat Money,
Which Does not Grow on Trees
With or Without the Bees.
They can Fly to the Moon
But they can't Feed the World,
You have to Ask About That...
Don't You? Don't You?
Food Really Does Grow on Trees,
But it does not Pick Itself.
Money Always Goes to Money,
We All Know That.
Don't We? Don't We?
They can take Ravens and Willow
Out of the Dictionary
But the Ravens still Caw their Warning
And the Willow still Weeps.

Avalon Blues

I can't find a rhyme for Avalon
Except a paltry Savalon.
I can't find one at all for Poetry
Unless you'll swallow Factory.
I want to write a Line or Two
About an Avalon Shade or Hue,
And the Fabulous Colours in the Sky,
Behind the Tor when its Wet or Dry.
But I must be feeling rather Wired,
As my Poem Tonight is a little Tired.
Try saying it in a Northern Tone,
And then it's getting in the Zone.
The Aries Moon is on the Wane,
Maybe that is why it's Lame.

Shattered

You Shattered my Dreams
Again and Again
Lovingly Yet
Ruthlessly, Mercilessly.

The Mountain I Climbed
Was not You
But My Very Own Self.

My Dolly Day Dreams Died
Over and Over.
The Mirror Cracked
Then Shattered
Smashed and Clattered
To the Ground of My Being.

Like Humpty Dumpty
I Spun Around Exhausted
Trying to Pick Up the Pieces
And Stick them Back Together
In a Clumsy Mosaic of my Life

Trying, Flailing, Failing
To Show You
The Intimate Wonder
Of Who I AM

But I AM Rohini
I AM Stubborn
And I AM Fixed
I AM Taurus in Ascendancy

I AM the Archer
I AM The Wings
I Move your Mountains
As I Sing to You

I Stare Stonily Into
The Angry Eye of the Bull
And Fix My Target
And Me Myself and I
And the Arrow
Which is God
Become One

The Stars are Dancing

Where have All the Flowers Gone?
Where are the Long Sunny Days and
Warm Sultry Nights?
Where are the Lovers
Kissing in Bowers?
Where is the Light
That I saw in Your Eyes?
Where is the Ancient Hope of the Nation?
Will Avalon be again on the Rise?

Our Beautiful Persephone
Has Picked her Last Flower
And Young Mary Magdalene
Is yet Safe in her Tower

All around seem Lost in Confusion
And the Latest Debate
Is on Fission or Fusion
While the Power Plant
Is Built by Greed and Delusion

Yet The Stars are Dancing
When I look out of my Window
They are Dancing
When I sing my Samhain Song
They are Dancing as I Shiver
With my Drum on the Hilltop

They are Dancing
When I close my Eyes
And Think of You

Excalibur; the Tongue

The Tongue, along with the Pen, Is THE
Mighty Sword
Of THIS Holy Temple;
The One Between your Ears
Not made with Human Hands,
But Fashioned in Silence
By the Most High, the Most Divine.

The Tongue is both the Body's Defender,
The Mind's Controller,
And the Soul's Builder.
It is Either the Worst Enemy
Or the Best Friend.

Be Ultra Careful with Words,
They are the Tools in our Kitbags,
With which we Fashion the Self,
Which will Eventually be Relinquished
Only when we have Understood
The Underlying Unity of All.

With Speech and Sound we Conjure
Ever New Magical Worlds into Being,
And Alone we will Inhabit them.

Make THIS World the Heaven
It was Intended to be.
Speak of what is Known,
Not of what is Believed.
Speak THIS New Heaven
And Earth into Being.

Listen to the Silence
And Allow it to Speak to you.
From It comes
The Music of the Spheres,
Creating Harmony
In All Things.

If you MUST Speak then
Don't Rattle and Endlessly Repeat,
For it is YOU who will be Stuck
In the Echo Chamber of your Own Mind.

If you MUST Write then don't Copy.
Don't Waste Words;
Make them True;
If they must be Harsh
Then also make them Fair.
Think Twice, Thrice,
Seven Times Seven,

Before Engaging Gob;
Consider; Is this Worth Saying?
Has it been Hashed and Rehashed Already,
A Million Times Before?
Am I Speaking to the Blind and the Deaf?

Or Am I the Echo to my Own Narcissus?
Am I Able to Listen too?
Are my Precious Words
A Waste of Holy Breath?
I Rest my Tongue with Relief
To Taste the Nectar Running Down
The Back of my Throat,
Then I Breathe Silently and Jump Joyfully
Into the Golden River of Life.

Make Words your Pearls;
And Thread a Necklace for your Neck
And a Girdle for your Waist.
Don't Cast them before Swine;
But Sing them with your Whole Heart
Into the Ears of Friends and Lovers.

Be Silent to your Enemies,
To Cavaliers and those with Ears of Cloth.
Use your Personal Excalibur

To Weed the Garden of the Self,
To Cut away the Bindweed of the Past
And thus Free YOUR World,
Not THE World, of Ignorance.

Bardic Blessing for Worthy Farm

In the Arms of God
Beyond Duality
There is Field
Where we can Meet

And I Will Meet You There

Beyond all Concepts
Of Good and Bad

And I Will Meet You There

It is Place
Where we can meet
Without the Sound
Of War's Defeat
Drumming and
Ringing in our Ears

While Some Play on
Our Hopes and Fears
And Manage All
Our Smiles and Tears

And I Will Meet You There

It's a Happy Place;
A Marvellous Field
It's Full of Gold
With a Healthy Yield

It Puts an End
To Sin and Shame
It's a Healing Balm
For all your Pain

And I Will Meet You There

It's a Lovely Field
Where Heavenly Cows
Graze in Meadows
Under Laden Boughs

Where Happy Sheep
Keep Watch at Night
Their Blackened Faces
Now in Light

Where your Friends
Are all your Peers
And the Crop is
Is Healthy
For Future Years

And I Will Meet You There

There is an Apple
On an Island In the
Middle of the Storm
There is a Tau
A Holy Cross,
It's in a Place
Quite near the Fosse

It's a Loving Field,
A Holy Plane,
Where all that Bull
You now can Toss

And Birth again
That Holy Cross
Upon which you
And I Are Born
In this New Field of
Heavenly Corn

To some it's known
As AVALON
The Isle of Apples
A Taurus Field
A Holy Temple
In Times of Need
And in the end
Our only Shield
A Sword in Battle
Against the Greed
A Place to Plant
That Holy Seed

And I Will Meet You There

May Worthy Farm and all the Worthies there,
Be Forever Blessed Henceforth
and Evermore

If You Want to Change the World First Love Yourself.

If you want to Change the World, First Change
Yourself.
Love Yourself, Really Love Yourself.

Find the Blazing Sun in your Chest
That Rises in the Deepest Darkness,
That Inspires you to Look Inside for the First
Time,
That Pierces the Veil of Illusion,
Brings you Crashing into the Moment,
And Melts and Caresses you into a Soft
Loving Blancmange of Effervescent Light.

Rise Above your Thoughts and Lower your
Eyelids
Feel the Blood and the Pulse of Life Rush
through you,
Smile Inwardly at No-one but the Ancient
Friend Inside you,
Feel the Force Within like a River of
Blossoms,

Carving New Faces in the Rocky Mountains of
your Mind.

If you want to Change the World Love
Yourself
Beyond all Fear of Humiliation and
Degradation,
Beyond your Fear of Being Burned or
Scorned,
Beyond All Reason and with Strong Resolve,
With Forgiveness but not Remorse in your
Heart.

If you want to Love Another first Love
Yourself,
Fiercely with White Hot Passion, Wildly,
With Gratitude for All that has been Given,
However Imperfect to your Outer Judging
Eyes.

Love your Wounds into Submission
And Bear your Scars with Well Deserved
Pride.
Listen to the Inner Voice Reminding you
Of your Need, not your Desire, for Fulfilment
And Let Freedom be your Home and Joy your
Prize.

Rise on Wings of Compassion and Kindness,
And Drink Great Draughts of the Waters of
Clarity,
Spiral into the Void with Certainty and
Sureness,
And Enjoy It's Loving Ephemeral Embrace.

Let the Embers of Disappointment Burn Out
And Raise the Fires of Glory and Sweetness,
Forgetting all Past Lives and Future
Possibilities.

Leave the Ashes of your Past where they Lie,
And Light Brave New Dancing Fires
In the Eyes of Others who also Seek Wisdom.
Do not Tremble or Weep before the Beloved,
Who IS you.....

But Welcome with Astonishment the I that you
Are,
And Allow any Tears to be of Relief and not
Bitterness.

Where you have been Lame, now Walk,
Where Stumbling; Stride, Where Shy;
Confident,
Where Lost; Found, where Barren; Fruitful,

Where Timid; Brave; where Desolate; Bloom,
Where Violated; Defiant, where Confused;
Clear,

Where Blind; now SEE.

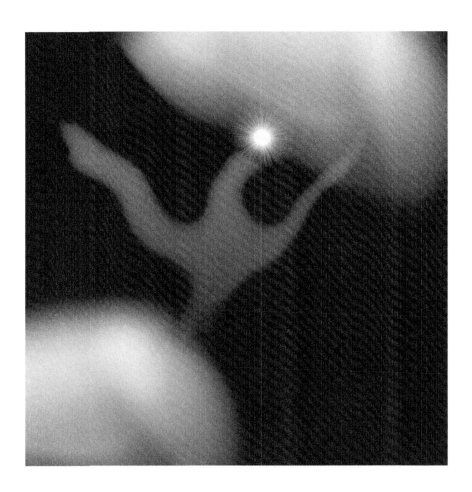

When You Come to Albion

When you come to Albion
I will plant an Ash tree in the garden
And we will walk in forest glades
And wear shirts of moss and lichen hue
And sit beside still water and gushing streams

When you come to Albion, I will wipe your feet
with my hair
And pocket the stars for your morning shower
And wrap you in fluffy towels after your
lakeside swim
And tell you to put on your winter vest
In case you should forget when frost is on the
grass

When you come to Albion I will laugh
Until the leaves shake down from the russet
oaks
And the echoes reach back from the furthest
stars

I will be your Santa Claus when Yuletide
comes
And Village Fires are lit
And we will be of good cheer despite our trials

I will show you joy out of suffering
And water out of sunlight
And stillness amidst the madness
I will share all of this with you, my Love,
When you come to Albion

Isolation Row

Getting to Know Me
Getting to Know All about Me
Getting to Like Me
Getting to Find I Like Me
Getting to Know Me
Putting It My Way but Nicely,
I AM Precisely
My Cup of Tea
Getting to know Me
Getting to Feel Free and Easy
When I AM with Me
There's Nothing to Say
Haven't I Noticed
Suddenly I AM Bright and Breezy
Because of All the Bea-utiful New Things to
See
Things I AM Learn-ing about Me
Day By Day
(HUM to self in the tune from The King and I)

I Don't Care

I don't care If you are Left or Right or Blue or
Red or Green
I don't care if you Love or Hate to be Seen on
any Scene
I don't care if you Like or don't Like Fresh or
Mouldy Cheese
Or Scraggy Cats or Cheapo Wine or Ugly
Dogs with Fleas

I don't care if your House is Owned or Shared
or Rented
Or if your Dusty Pot Pourri is Pachouli or
Lemon Scented
I don't care where you take your Coveted
Vacations
Or if you go to Pubs or stay at Home for
Lubrications

I don't care which Denomination of Church or
Mosque you Like
Or if you Travel around by Car or on a
Rackety Old Bike

I don't care what you Believe, it means you just don't Know
I don't care if you are Stuck, it means you cannot Flow

I don't care if Scorpio Saturn is in your Seventh House
I don't care if you're a Man a Woman or a Little Mouse
I don't care if you're a Denier or if you're a Climateer
But I care if you're an Oil Rapist to keep the Oil Price Dear

I don't care if they call the World a Globe as long as it's not a Ploy
To keep us all Distracted while they treat us all as Toys
To Keep us Down, to keep us Quiet, to Keep us without Joy
And under Tight Control Like Good Little Girls and Boys

I don't care if you're a Banker as long as you don't Fleece
The very vast majority who truly just want Peace
I don't care if you think the World is Flat or

Round or Square
BUT I care if you are Loaded because you cannot Share

I care if you are Kind and I care that you have Peace
I care about the Animals, and I care about the Trees
I care about the Birds and I care about the Bees
I care about the Old Ones who are brought down to their Knees

I care about the Children Wiped out in all the Wars
I care about the Lies we're told as they Settle Filthy Scores
I care about Injustice and I care about the Oceans
I care that we have Real Green Herbs and not just Filthy Potions

I care that Art and Music and all the Heavenly Letters
Are not kept Solely for Public Schools with their Henrys and Henriettas

I care that you have Happiness and I hope
that Love will Flow
I care that in the Earth to come we all will
come to KNOW

The Female Warrior of the Rainbow

It is a tough road, this one.
You will be hated for your failures,
But equally for your successes.

You will be put on pedestals
Only to be knocked off them.

You will be hated
For the ridiculous;
For being spotty,
Too tall, too pretty, too ugly,
Too clever, too stupid,
Too intelligent,
Too talented.

Too rich, too poor.

The wrong colour.

You will be hated
For being too loud,
And for being too silent,
And for daring to sing your song.

You will be hated for your body,
For being too fat or too thin,
Too old, too ill, too healthy.

You will be criticized for
Being too harsh,
And too soft,
Too kind, yet too cruel.

You must be evil,
You must be possessed?
You will be scourged by those
You have helped and loved.

This is the Way of the Female Warrior.
Know it. Internalise it. Heal it.
Rise to it.

Love them all anyway.

You will be hated for shining a light
On truths that wish to hide
Behind the shield of darkness
And clever lies.
You will be betrayed
In places High and Low,
And will find forgiveness in your heart.

In this you will find
Sweet release and Divine freedom.

You will smile within,
Hold your peace,
Know your God,
Find the Inner Kingdom,
When the Outer has failed you,
Throw the lies to the seven winds,
And Kiss the critics goodbye

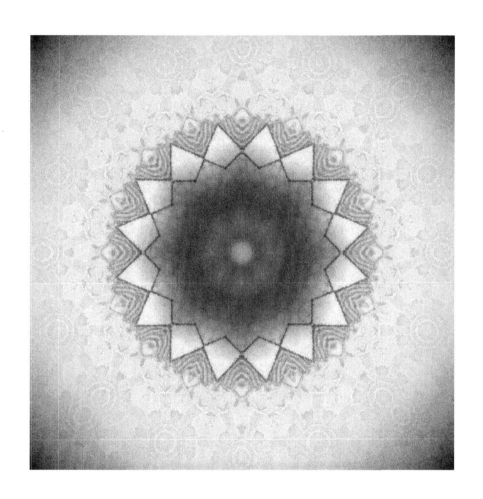

Dance with Divinity

Cake or Cherries?
Porridge or Cornflakes?
Decisions, Decisions.......
Whether with Precision
Or Derision
The Subtle and Blunt
Surgeon's Knife
Of Eternal Life
Cuts Away Delusions
And All Illusions
With a Merciless Hack
Or a Subterranean Slice.

Science is Useful
But Mostly Poppycock
You Know That
You KNOW That.......

Simon Says
Put your Hands on Your Head
Boris Says OK
Jesus Says Don't Do It
Buddha Smiles
Krishna Says Nothing at All.

Crucifixion as Symbolism
Has Bypassed the Masses;
Was Always Meant to be of Sense
Not of All Feeling.

"Civilized" Barbarism
Crucifies the Gnostic Christ
In Us All Every Day,
With Lurid Headlines
We Lap Up Stupidly
Like Pussy Cats with Cream,
Or Rabid Dogs
Ravenously Devouring Carcasses
From Ancient Carcassonne.

Eros? Thanatos?
The West End
Is the Best End?
The East End
And Anteros
Is a Better Blend
My Dearest Friend.

Unveiling Isis
Cannot be Done by Thieves
Or Thuggery.

Life Does not Begin
In a Test Tube.

Simon Says Sit DOWN!

I Say NO!
My Spirit Rebels.
Give me Some Truth!

I SAY;
Dance with Divinity,
Ride a Wild Horse,
Laugh Like a Child,
Fly on the North Wind,
Enough IS Enough,
Leave This Nonsense Behind.

Know Thyself.

Day Forty-Six of Staying In

Are you Staying off the Gin?
Are you Pulling out your Hair?
Are you Saying a Desperate Prayer?
Are you Doing your Daily Yoga
In your Knickers or Flowery Toga?
Are you Mowing the Chamomile Lawn
Finding it All a Terrible Yawn?
Are you Missing the Local Takeaway
Or your Annual Vital Sunny Breakaway?
Are you Driving your Loved Ones Crazy?
Are you Being Awfully Lazy?
Are you Diving in the Fridge?
Are you up the Tor with your Drum or Didge?
Are you Watching the Wesak Moon?
Playing Buddha a Birthday Tune?
Is it Hugh Grant AGAIN on the Telly
While you Add to your Buddha Belly?
Notting Hill, with a Box of Chocs....
On Messenger with that Shakti Fox!
Are you Happy Despite it All?
Are you Managing to have a Ball?
When your Party is Inside
You'll have a Fabulous Wesak Ride.
Meditate, Levitate, Tune In Tune Out
That is what it's All About

The Dove of Peace

I Walk the Abbey Grounds
Where All the Stones are Thrown Down
As was Written
And the Jaws of the Whale are a Reminder
Of the Sign of Jonah
And There you Still Are
Little White Dove
Where the First Wattle Church was Built
In This Sacred Holy Land
You have the Wings of Love
Wrapped Around my Lonely Heart
You are the Holy Spirit
And you are My Mother Still
Giving Wings to my Dreams

They Are Over; the Days of Wine and Roses...

They Seemed so Long
The Mad Dog Days of
Weeping and Laughter;
The Timeless Torrid Loves;
The Horny Hours and
Desperate Agonies
Of Unquenched and
Unfulfilled Desire;
The Days of Uncontrollable
Unmanageable Hatreds;
Thankfully all Dissolving Now
Before the Golden Gate
Beyond the Bridge of Sighs.

They are Now Over,
The Days of Wine and Roses,
The Ones my Lover brought me,
When I was Still in Kindergarten.
Clarity has replaced the Claret
In this New Waking Dream,
Where Now only Wild Dog Roses
Scramble in Humming Hedgerows,
And no longer Wilt as Specimens
On my Suburban Windowsill

The Wending Wobbly Way is Open,
The Nectar Slides Slowly Down
My Slackened Thorny Throat
As Sweet as Baby's Breath,
My Cracked and Humbled Heart
Is Truly, Madly, Deeply Thankful
In this Strange and Marvellous Dream...........
Within a Dream......Within a Dream.....

I'm Really Really Sorry; You Don't Know How Sorry I Am

You have to Know I Feel Remorse
For Ancient Karma's Misused Force
This Body Temple has been Wracked
By Realisations Tortuous Fact

This Body Amour Made of Steel
Is Searching for A Way to Heal
The Split of Lower and Higher Mind
Has Danced Through Seasons Most Unkind

Harnessing the Once Blind King
Has Seen a Time of Suffering
But Now the White and Winged Horse
Allays old Suffering in its Course

The Battlefield of Mind Delayed
The Sun's True Rising Unallayed
And the Pearl of Wisdom Plucked Not
While the Mind Retained Its Spot

The Diamond Sutra Taught a Cure
Of How to Make an old Mind Pure
And Now New Seasons Come to Mind
Remorse Has left the Past Behind
Each Moment Shines with Blessed Grace
Towards my God I Turn my Face

The End Days

These are the End Days
The Let us Not Pretend Days
The Days for Study
In Wild Waters Muddy
Of the Cabal or Kabbalah
Of Hell or Valhalla
Are OVER Now
You Chose your Holy Cow
You Milked Her, You Ate her
Now do not Berate Her
If the Eyes in your Head
Just Fill you with Dread
The Single Eye Escaped You?
The Left Eye Just Raped You?
Your Wife Just Left You?
Your Children Hate You?
A Virus Just Felled You?
Algorithms Just Spelled You?
Al Gore Just Repelled You?
Know Thyself and the War
Within Will be Over
The Battle Lines Drawn
For a New Dusk; a New Dawn

I Still Love You

I love you for all the men
I have and have not known
I love you for all the time
I have and have not lived
For sea salt and beach love
For the snowdrops braving the
Last bite of winter
For rescuing the animals tortured in battery
farms
And the horses, cats and dogs I have loved
purely
I love that your compassion is courageous
I love that you love
I love that your teeth are like sheep
Your hair like goats
And you have dove eyes within your locks
I love that others do not understand us
I love our secret silent language

I love you for the men I have never met
Who I have despised
You reflect me and now I see myself
The desert gave way to the quicksand and the
mountain
Long ago and today meet in this moment
called NOW
The deaths I crossed on straw and crawling
Have pierced the wall of my mirror
And forgotten words are now remembered
As I learn to live life
Your wisdom not mine you have shared with
me
On an open loan
And I have swallowed it
I love you beyond illusion
For the immortal heart I now possess
I no longer doubt
As knowledge has grown palaces of light
You are still the Great Sun
And I am still drunk
When I am sure of me

The Wisdom of Pegasus

(Salm is the Star in the middle of the Square
of Pegasus, the middle decan of Aquarius. It
is where the word Psalm comes from and is
also the root of Salmon, and the Salmon of
Wisdom, which is numerologically a 9, for
completion)

May you Never be Hungry
May you always have at Least One Friend
May you Never Lay your Head Down
Without a Warm Bed or a Hand to Hold
May you always be Happy and Never
Deceived
May your Right Arm be Strong
And your Left Brain Reigned In
May you Learn the Knowledge from Elders
And Tend the Bounty of Mother Earth
May you Receive each Breath in Gratitude
And each Heartbeat in Awareness
May the Divine Mother Rise up inside you
And Birth the Divine Child within you
May you Awaken to Brave New Worlds
And Bright Universes of Joy

May you End Old Contracts of Hurt and Pain
And Stay Generous in the Face of Greed
And Stalwart in the Face of Danger
May you be Kind in a World of Madness
And Strong in the Face of Adversity
May your Loneliness make you Indomitable
And your Meditation make you Whole
May Understanding Replace your Beliefs
And May Love Rule your World
And the Green Futures of your Children
May the Cows Return Home
To their Safe Taurus Fields
And the Love for the Animals be Remembered
in Eden
May the Wool be Removed from your Eyes
And the Veil be Lifted from your Heart
May the Wisdom of Pegasus Guide you
And May the North Star Lead you Home

Not Yet

Are we Ready for the New World,
Dressed as she is, with Flowers Unfurled?
Like the Bride that she is, for Love not for
Duty,
Blessed with her Taurean Venusian Beauty?

The Sun Rises and Sets, and Rises and Sets,
Then Rises and Sets and Rises AGAIN,
And Again and Again and Again and Again,
And Again and Again and Again and
Again.......

And That Might Sound Like Really Old Hat
But they've Sold you a Zillion Stories of That,
And Built a World Based on Power and Gain,
While we Swallowed the Ancient Set Refrain.

Are we Ready, then or Not?
Will you Look Back like the Wife of Lott?
Or Put your hand to the Heavenly Plough,
And Once and for all Kick that Holy Cow.....?
Two Words will Stay with Me and Yet,
I will Nourish Hope and not Regret,
The Two Words that will Stay, you Bet?
Sadly they are " Not Yet". Not Yet.

La Belle Dame avec Merci

O None can Ail thee my Proud Knight
Nor yet Alone nor Pale
The Birds are Singing on the Lake
And the Spiralling Sedge is Withered not

I know what Ailed thee my Once Knight in
Arms
You were Haggard and Woe-Begone
But the Squirrel's Granary is now Full
And the Harvest is Truly Done

I see a Lily as your Crown
No Anguish nor Fever left to Burn
I see in your Heart a Blooming Rose
That can Surely never Fade

You Once met a Lady in the Meadow
As Beautiful as a Faery Child
With Flowing Hair and Light of Foot
And Wildness in her Eyes

You set her on your Swiftest Steed
And thought of Nothing Else at All
She Sang a Sweet yet Siren's Song
To Lead you to her Rocks

You made a Garland for her Hair
You Wound Bracelets of Gold upon her Wrists
She Smelled of Violets as she Moaned
And Spoke False Words of Love

She fed you on Truffles and Caviar
And the Taste of Honey was on her Lips
You took it for the Manna Blessed
As she said She Loved you True

She took you to her Sleepy Grotto on the Hill
Where she Gazed at you and Sighed
You Shut her Sad Wild Eyes with Kisses
As you and your Lady Fell Asleep

Side by Side upon the Moss
You Slept and Dreamed a Dream of Woe
That Hill was Cold and Drear and Bleak
As Arthur still Slept in his Sad Cave

You Saw the Pale Rider, Kings and Princes
Warriors that were Once Yourself
They Cried out to the Lady without Mercy
Who had you in her Thrall

You Saw their Starving Lips in the Gloom
Gaping and Thirsting in Horrid Warning
Then you Woke and Found you were still Here
On the Cold and Threatening Tor

And this is why I Sojourn here
Though not Alone nor Loitering
The Sedge Returns from its Withering
And the Birds are Singing Loud and Strong

The Blossom will soon be on the May
And the Pole will surely Flip
You will Find a Belle Dame avec Merci
Upon the Hillside's Sunny Banks

So come and join the Happy Throng
And Throw your Sorrows to the Winds
There's Real Manna when you Know to Look
Now Put Aside that Holy Book

It's Work for you is Done

****

I Miss Seeing Your Face

Do you Remember my Love
When I Planted Snowdrops
Under the Oak Tree
Outside Our Kitchen Window?
We Planted Daffodils too
And Tulips from Amsterdam
But the Slugs Ate them
Such a Beautiful Garden we Lived in
I Fell in Love with you there
Amidst Purple, Pink and White
Rhododendrons
And Yellow Honeysuckle
We Planted Magnolias and Willows
And a Monkey Puzzle Tree

We Planted a Rose for Greta called Bliss
Dahlias and Foxgloves
Orange Nasturtiums, Pansies and Violets
And Red Geraniums
My Red Hot Pokers were Trampled by
Builders
But your Potted Palms did Well

We Buried Abigail Angel Toes
Under the White Hydrangea
And my White Wisteria Blossomed
Only After you had Died
And I had Left

So much Love went into that Garden
But it is Gone Now
Cruelly Bulldozed for Profit
All that is Left is an Old Empty Mansion
And a Tired Old Lilac Wisteria
No one Else will Fall in Love
With it or in it Now
But it will Always be Ours
With the Pine Trees and Bracken
And Majestic Oaks

Do you Remember the Fairy Ring at the
Bottom
Going Down to the Lake?
The Emerald Moss we Bounced Upon
Near to where Bonfires were Lit?
The Swimming Pool Overlooking
A Beautiful Smooth Lawn
Where Once a Lama Sat
And Wild Parties were Held?

We held our Wedding Reception
In a White Marquee
On the Happiest Day of my Life
So Far

I Loved Everyone that Day
And you Shone Brightly
In my Heart's Sky
It Took Two Valium
To get you Down the Aisle
And there was a Divine Madness
About that Day
Mixing all the Friends and Relations
And the Mayors from Slough
Into an Unlikely Cocktail

It came together Haphazardly
Into a Wonderful Whole
I have Many Vignettes in my Soul
From that Day
Too Many to Write Here
They would Fill a Book
Which Maybe One Day I Will Write
I didn't Know That Day
The Tragedies that would Follow
And that was Just as Well

I Was to Lose you Cruelly
Before we Lived Out
A Comfy Retirement with Slippers
I had in all Truth
Lost you before you Left
I Think you were Lost to Yourself
And that's the Reason
It all went so Pear Shaped
As you would Say
But there isn't a Day goes by
When you aren't with me
And you are Still
The Main Love of my Life

You were my only Husband
Out of a Rather Mixed Bag
What am I Supposed to do Now?
Write a Bunch of Turgid Poems?
I Withdrew from the World
When you had Gone
Licked my Wounds
And Nearly came after you
I Feel I Let you Down
When we knew you were Dying
I was Broken Myself
And I could not Heal you

I did not have in my Armory then
The Sacred Holy Herb
And you Believed too much
In the Medics
Or so I now Believe

I have to Accept
That you went when it was your Time
And I had Still much to Learn
That had to be Done without you
There has been some Joy
In the Learning
Although there have been
Painful Revelations
That would Probably Never
Have Occurred had you Lived

There Must be a Rhyme
And a Reason to it all
But the Upshot is
That I am Alone Now
Or at Least not in
A One to One Relationship
I don't Wake Up to Cups of Tea
That you Brought me in Bed
I Still Hear you Saying

That Life has no Guarantees
And I have Found that to be Almost True

I'll be Honest and Say
That I don't Miss the Drinking
But I Miss the Kindness
In your Eyes
And the Walks by the River
The Country Pubs
And the Mad Dinner Parties
I Miss you at Family Gatherings
At Christmas
And I don't go Travelling any More
You got the Travel Bug
Out of my System

I Miss your Hard Work
And your Diplomacy
And your Loving Embrace
I Miss your Body
And your Strong Tattooed Arms
But Most of All
I Miss Seeing your Face

****

Beatitudes with Attitude

"Blessed are the Poor in Money but not in
Spirit,
for yours is the Kingdom of the Heaven
WITHIN.
"Blessed are the Wealthy who share your
Wealth,
for yours is the Rightful Governance of
Albion."
"Blessed are the Whistle Blowers
and those who Call Time on War"
"Blessed are the Truth Seekers,
and the She Punks who are Avenged not
Revenging,
who Eat their Dish Cold and with Laughter
Rejoicing"
"Blessed are those who Mourn Unseen,
for you are Comforted by the Lovers of Life."
"Blessed are the Meek and the Gypsy
Singers,
for you are Inheriting our Mother the Jewel our
Earth.
"Blessed are you who Hunger and Thirst
for Righteousness and Real KNOWLEDGE,
for you ARE Filled with the Aquarian Waters
of Life."

"Blessed are the Merciful,
for you are given Mercy in Buckets not Bucket Lists."
"Blessed are the Pure in Heart,
for you ARE seeing God not in Buildings but in Human Hearts."
"Blessed are the Peacemakers,
for you ARE called The Children of Light"
"Blessed are you who are Persecuted
for Righteousness by Stupidity,
for yours IS the Kingdom of the Heaven WITHIN."
"Blessed are you when people Insult you,
Persecute you and Falsely say all Kinds of Evil against you,
and you Smile and Walk away Blessing not Cursing."
"Blessed are you who take Right Action in the Face of Twats and Users, for you are Inviolate"
"Blessed are the Servers of all Brothers and Sisters of Earth
and not the Worshipful Company of DIM."
"Rejoice and be Glad, because Great is your Reward NOW,

For in the same way they Persecuted The Truth Speakers and Peace Brokers who were before you,
Still they do it now in the name of their Man Made gods and Idols in their Houses of Beautiful Empty Cold Stone."
"Blessed are you who Notice your Breath and Receive the Blessings Therin."

There Endeth The Lessons."

When I Am Free

When I am Free
I go where the Wind takes me.
It Licks me like a Lover
Above the Sun's Hot Kisses.

When I am Free
The Roaring Rain Lashes me
And the Gentle Drops Tickle
And Wash me Clean.

When I am Free
The Mother Earth Cradles me,
She Rocks me and she Feeds me
As she Births and Swallows me
Anew Each Day.

When I am Free
The Father Sky
Looks down and Cracks
A Happy, Aloofish Smile.

When I am Free
The Fairies Dance
And Laugh for Joy,

And on a Clear Summer Night
All the Crazy Canopy of Stars
Come out to Play.

Good Morning

Here is my Mourning Poem about Blake (who
I did not know personally)

Blake. He was a Little Bloke.
He Carried a Yoke.
Liked a Good Joke.
Gave the Fires of Albion a Jolly Good Stoke.

Sorry, it's the best I can do at this time of the
Mourning

The Return of the Christ

The Wheel Turns and Will.
Yet THIS TIME the Falcon hears the Falconer.
Orion's Big Dog Rips the Heart from
Unknowing
While the Little Dog Trots Faithfully at his
Master's Heels

Things Come Together; the Centre Holds
Anarchy has Always been a Loose Thing
Yet the Ceremony of Innocence is Revival
The Best Always had Conviction
Though the Worst are Still Full of Passionate
Intensity
And for all that, they are Never Still.

The Revelation IS at Hand.
Was Always at Hand.
The Second Coming?
Have you not Seen It?

The Vast Image out of Spiritus Mundi
The Thirsting and Hunger
For Lack of the Knowledge
Those Waters of Life
Which Water the Desert and Open the Eye

Did you Miss that?

That Shape of the Lion's Body with the
Woman's Head
That Sphinx and her Riddles
The Ages between Virgo and Leo

The Universal Virgin Birth
Around Precession
To the Return of the King.

Is DONE. Dusted and Revealed as Universal
Truth.

Have you Seen It?
Have you Seen It?

The Pitiless Gaze, the Blank Stare
Were once your Own and your Reflection.
Now your Beauty is Revealed.
That was always THE Revelation.

The Swallows Wheel
But the Paired Eagles
Spiral Freely towards the Infinite Sun.
Burning, Burnished, and Joyful

The Darkness Drops at Night
Twenty Centuries of Sleep
Are Roused from Nightmares
To Sonorous Sanguine Tangerine Dreams

The Rough Beast that Slouched in You
Following Horus around that Clock of Hours
Has Arrived in Bethlehem
At the Zenith of your Life
In That Moment Out of Time
And is Born Anew.

The Lack of Assumptions of the Virgin Mind

I want to Know you from a Clear Place.
A Virginal Place.

I'll Talk to Anyone, me.
I don't Prejudge or take upon myself
The Assumptions of others.

I won't Lie down so you can Trample over me
Or Seduce me with Clever Lies or even Wine
and Roses,
But I might Lay a while in the Long Grass
And Speak Silently with you of Love.

We don't have to be Lovers in the Physical
Realms
Although that Possibility Exists,
With all other Possibilities.....
But we can Watch the Waves
On Brighton Beach
Or catch our Breath together
On the Windy Downs.

We can walk in Silent Woods
And Sit under Gnarly Trees

And Listen to the Birds
And Follow them in Flight.

We can Put down all the Yesterdays
Where we were Mistaken,
And Only JUST Missed the Mark,
As The Eye of the Bull
Takes a Steady Aim
And a Constant Heart,
Which comes ONLY from Diligent Practice.

The Virginal Mind Assumes Nothing.
Takes on no Baggage or Prejudice.
Is Unveiled, Stripped and Quivering.

READY.

To Understand Something?

That is surely the Goal,
And when you do?

Nothing will Stop you Now.

Talking to God

When all Around me
Are Against me
And the Night is Long
And Friends have Deserted me
When the Children are Still Dying
And the Most Beloved are all Dead
I Will not Give Up

When the Trees are Burning
And Governments Crashing
I will not Falter for thy Strength
Is in my Right Hand O God

The Very Dragons
Of this Great Land
Have Protected me
And the Guardian Spirits
Have Welcomed me
In their Lairs
And Private Sanctuaries
The Fairies have Spoken
And the Angels have
Wiped my Tears Away

When I have been Used,
Abused and Lied about
I have Triumphed,
For my Will is Pure
And Tested with Fire
My Integrity is Intact
My Armour is the Light
My Sword is the
Sword of Truth
Which Hurts No-one

The Trees Sing to me
Their Sacred Songs
And the Grasses Dance
For me in the Breeze
The Sun Kisses me
With Her Warmth
And the Inner Fire
Cannot be put Out
By the Betrayals of Mere Men
Or Women

My Heart is a Lion's Heart
My Eyes are Eagle's Eyes
And the Bull of my Ego
Is Restrained
And Dying Daily

The Water Man has Come
And my Courage
Has not Failed Me

When Men and Women
Have Doubted Me
I have Stood Firm in the Light
And I will Stand Alone in it
For as Long as You Ask Me
Mother/Father God

On Cigarettes and Whisky

Breach born kneeling and coughing
In the bitter winter
You learned young not to expect anything of
life
But not to wait without hope
For mercy's kiss
The staring perfect doll's eyes
Were already dead
Before you laid them down to sleep

You and I wrote so many words
In and out of the asylum
I recalling my grandmother's death in Bedlam
And you remembering private slings and
arrows
And the Destiny of the Briar Rose

There were nights of excess
Of cigarettes and whisky
And Wild Wild Women

And Wild Men come to that
We were both women of zeal and greed
For life in all its giddy panorama
There were many other qualities
Too many to list here

But zealotry didn't work out for me or you in
the end
Peering into the mirror
Was an almost impossible effort
For you and I

I too saw the drunken rat
But she disappeared as I caught
Her tail spinning on illusion's wheel

You knelt in hope of mercy's kiss
Did she ever come?
Perhaps not

Yet I no longer kneel or plead
As she puckered up for me
Just in the Nick of Time

So Many Me's

There's Little Me
And Big Me
Soppy Me
Weepy Me
Sexy Me
Youthful Me
Pretty Me
Ugly Me
Ancient Me
Invisible Me
Happy Me
Furious Me
No Way Twee Me
All the Me's
Of the Choppy, Angry
Deluded, Excluded
Sat On Shat On
Loved with Hat On
Violent And Calm
Piscean Seas

My Me

I LOVE YOU ME!

For Paula

You remind me of the ocean covered with
whitecaps
And you Know how to say No
You may once have been a woman entering a
convent
And an Officer preparing to drill his men
Also I see a man declared Bankrupt
And I think you were a woman of Sumeria
You know how to breakthrough to a new
spiritual level
I see you on a Houseboat on the Nile
Peering over your Glasses
Learning how to Say Yes

Me and John

The other day
I met John Lennon
On the Inner Plane
And we had a barbecue
In my back garden
Surrounded by happy silent children

I thought "the wonder that I feel is easy"
I was wearing a long sixties style dress
And a translucent body
And a black hat with
Wide brim and a black rose

We didn't speak until he left
He said
I would kiss you but your breath smells
Which I could have taken
As an ego blow
But I didn't
I laughed
But I did resolve
To use a better mouthwash
Than Listerine Next time

I AM a Walk in the Garden of the Tuileries

AM a Flock of Wild Geese
I AM a Deep-Sea Diver
I AM a Fat Boy Mowing the Lawn
I AM A Big White Dove
I AM a Messenger Bearer
I AM an Orangutan
I AM a Two Men and A Woman
Castaway on a Small Island
In the South Seas
I AM a Walk in the Garden of the Tuileries

In Life after Life

From distraction to distraction
We wander and wonder
And we miss the peace
In this Holy Spirit of breath
Given freely to all of us
Under the Sun

We stand divided and dividing
In all our religions
Disempower our women
Who brought us forth into life
We miss the fiery love in our temple
Bestowed upon all on the wings of the dove

Escaping the Mire

Affairs can be Torrid
But also Horrid
And Marriage is Often
An Empty Carriage
But Love is a Dove
That Hovers Above
And Gives your Flings
A Pair of Wings
To Escape the Mire?
A Chariot of Fire

The Quenching

I AM a Dragon Cloud
I AM a Mossy Forest Pool
I AM the Dove and Raven
I AM the Prison and the Haven
I AM the Earthly School

I AM Sadness
I AM Happiness
I AM the Goldfish and the Lark
I AM the Whole Nine Yard's
I AM Old Noah's Ark

I AM Alice
I AM Guinevere
I AM the Smile Upon your Lips
I AM ARTHUR
I AM JESUS
I AM Moses and King Tut
I AM Everywhere and Nowhere
I AM Every AND and BUT

I AM the Branch
I AM the Vine
I AM Ash and Oak
And Pine

I AM your Holy Breath
I AM the Water
I AM the Blood and Wine

I AM the Best
I AM the Worst
I AM the Hunger
I AM the Thirst

I AM the Agony
And the Wrenching

BUT for You
Especially for YOU

I AM the Manna
AND the
Quenching

The Stone of Destiny

From the Mirror's Clear Refraction
Springs True Good and Radiant Action,
Not from Busy Hustle Bustling
Or Willy Nilly Noisy Hammering.

It Grows on Silent Mountains
In Happy Hippocrene Memory Fountains;
Out of Dangerous Ravines
From Solitude in Verdant Greens,
From Slings and Arrows of Desire
And Sorrows Purified by Fire.

It Grows from Sufferings Unknown,
It Grows when we Learn to be Alone;
From the Pains Untold and Undeserved,
From the Years of Never being Heard.

It Leaps up from the Dragons Tooth;
From Terror, Lies, and Old Untruths,
It Grows on Summits of Snow and Ice,
It Grows from Toads and Roaring Mice.

It Grows not from the Pages of Vogue
But in the Cauldrons of Meeks Gone Rogue.

Destiny Leads to the Magic Stone,
Only in Solitude; Completely Alone;
Not from Poets Blithe or TV Shows
But Destiny in Silence Grows.

It Grows from Leaving the Lonely Herd,
And Nourishing the Inner Word.
It Grows Not by a Babbling Brook,
Or Fairy Tales in Story Book.

It Grows not from Knocking on a Hollow Door,
Or from Marrying into Rich or Poor.

It Ties Itself to No-one's Strings,
It Acts Alone and Summons Wings.
It Finds its Peace in Peace Itself,
Not Sitting Waiting on a Shelf.

Away and Far from the Madding Crowd,
Is Right Action Hatched and Love Allowed.
In Solitude with Friendly Stars and Spheres
There is the Path that Destiny Reveres

Mary Potter

The End of Pisces
The End of Illusions
The Parting of the Veil
The End of Delusions

The End of Being
All Lost at Sea
Both Astrologically
And Literally

It was not Jesus and Harry
It was Jesus and Mary
Divine Male and Female
So What is So Scary?

El is Electric;
The Male in his Power
Mag is Magnetic;
Mary in her Tower

It's in us ALL
Whether Gay or Straight
But you Still have to Walk
Alone through the Gate

The Wheel is Turning
Well, *some* knew it Would
And in the End
It's For your Own Good

If you've not Yet Read
The Signs of the Times
Perhaps it's Time that you Do?
Will you Be One
Of the Hand Wringing Many?
Or Will you Be
One of the Happiest Few?

It's Just a Suggestion
Don't Get Indigestion

But Did you Think
The Crock you were Sold
Was Ever Going
To Turn to Real Gold?

Revelations are Always
Mocked and Shocking
Or they Would not be
Revelations but
Hooey or Hocking

It was Just a Scam
But it Seemed to Work
They were Just Phishing....
So Stop Being a Jerk

It's Time to Stand Up
And Say "I AM Alive"
I Belong to God/Goddess
I was Meant to Thrive

"I was Born Alive
And Alive I Be"
The Name you Wrote Down
Was Not Really Me

I was Born not Birthed
By Air was Inspired
I was Loved then Earthed
Then Watered and Fired

Mary Potter's my Name
Real Love is my Game
There will be Restitution
For the Faked Prostitution

I AM Mary the Magnetic
I AM Mary the Magdalene
I AM Mary the Divine Mother
I AM Mary the Moon
I AM Mary the Ocean
I AM Mary the Virgin Queen
I AM So much more Powerful
Than Electricity

Why Aren't you Laughing?
You will Laugh Yet

I AM MARA the Bitter One
From my Bitterness and Pain
Is Born the Child of Promise
From my Charisma is
Born the Christ in YOU

I was a once Babe in
My Mother's Arms
She Tried to Protect
Me from All Harms
But I, Like you
Was Cast on the Ocean
To Return to Source God
Through REAL Love and Devotion

I AM ELECTROMAGNETIC
TRULY PROPHETIC
I AM AND SO ARE YOU
FOR YOU AND I ARE THAT
I AM THAT I AM THAT I AM THAT I AM

The Magdalene Maligned

The Morning Star Rises
She Has Your Face
You Reach for Heaven
And Down with Grace
Your Starfire Burns
But Not All Yet See
Your Womanly Charms
As Your Purity

Rennes le Chateau's
Five-Pointed Star
Leads Outwards and Upwards
To Where you Are
For Thousands of years
You've been Shrouded in Mystery
Now the Cathars are Back
To Right Wrongful History

Your Place As a Woman
So Long So Derided
Is Restored Before God
Yin and Yang Undivided

Your Star Temple Is Here
By the Mountain's it's Signed
Once Again in this Age
Earth and Heaven Aligned

Solomon's Seal
Three Times in the Sky
Can be Read By The Pure
That the Lord is Nigh
The Earth's Crying Out
To be Cleansed of Our Crimes
Let Us Hope for the World
We Get it Right in These Times

Remember Monsegur

Remember Monsegur
And the Sacrifice of the Pure
The Rage of the Unholy Church Unleashed
On the Voice of Truth and Love and Peace

The Bird Tribes Return to
The Burning Ground
From All Corners of the Earth
In This Age
Reconciliation, Cleansing
Acceptance, Remembrance
Of the parts We all have Played
The Goods
The Bads

The Release from the Pendulum Swing of
Duality
No More "What I did to You"
Or "What you did to Me"
We did Each Other No Real Harm Thank God

The Grail King Lives Forever
We Have Not Forgotten
In the Sweet Fire
Of His Heart

We Burn Joyously
Remember Monsegur
And Give Thanks
For His Return

The End is Not Nigh; It Never Was!

Forget the Doom Mongers, The Naysayers,
And the Toothless Ruthless Soothsayers,
The TV Hacks and Bottom Feeders,
The Users, Takers and Grotty Leaders,
The Greedy, The Weedy, The Downright
Seedy,
The Holier than Thou In your face Creedy,
The Sneering, Leering, Electioneering,
Hopeless, Pointless Entitled Peering,
The Warring Whoring in Parliament Snoring,
Red Faced, Red Necked Politicians Boring.

For Around your Head Dance Twelve Bright
Stars,
While you Celebrate the Marriage of Venus
and Mars,
And you Raise the Solar Plexus' Sun
To its Rightful Place of Love and FUN,
And at your Feet is the Crescent Moon,
While Muses Sing their Heavenly Tune,
And Gaia Gives up her Scented Fruits

To the Sound of Holy Harps and Lutes,
The Breeze is Light and the Grasses Dance,
Not from a Mills and Boon "Romance",
But to the Singing of Perpetual Choirs,

And Kindling the Phoenix' Kindly Fires,
And the Moon Shaped Scythe of Father Time
Can Touch you no more in Rhythm nor
Rhyme.

Stop the Clocks

Time has been Called at Last
And the Clocks have Stopped.
The Princess Pricked her Finger,
The Spinning Wheel of Dharma was Spun,
And was Kicked into Rickety Reverse.

The Juggernaut of Ego Shuddered
And Screeched to a Grinding HALT!
After Aeons Asleep and Separated
The Prince of Peace Arrived
Handsome and Bang on Time
On his Snowy White Horse. Of Course!

The Invitations for the Divine
Wedding Banquet of the Lamb
Have been Sent out by Email,
Rather than on Guilded Paper,
And have been Rudely Refused
But also Graciously Accepted.

Then The Hammer Hit the Anvil,
The Nine Rivers Flowed into the Sea,
The Angel Poured out the Wrath Daily
On the Unready and Unsuspecting,

And the Heavenly Cup Overflowed
With Joy, Love and Delight.

The Dove Returned to the Argo,
And the Holy Ship Turned Around,
And Headed for the Brighter Shores……..

The Return to our Source
Became Only in this Age of NOW
A Manageable Possible Choice,
As It Always Was in Fact!!
As It was only Ever NOW!
No Bargains with the Devil here,
Only Vindication and Victory!

Yet Rabbits Run into their Holes,
Foxes Remain Cunning and Sly,
Politicians Prevaricate and Befuddle,
And Cry "The End is Nigh"
Like they Always did!

The Night Watchmen are all still Asleep.
Yet Your Hand is Firmly on the Plough,
And the Seals are Broken.
Altair and Vega continue their Love Story
Unhindered by The Milky Way,
Or Dreamy Distant Longings,

Or Unrequited Foamy Forgetting

Illusion Bit and was Gulped Down Whole,
Like the Sun Swallowing the Moon!
Now The Great Bear and the Little Bear
Are Asking you to Arise again TALITHA!

Fire Running In Your Veins

If you Gave All you Had
But are Rejected,
While there's Breath
In your Body
Walk Away.

If you've been Judged and Ridiculed
Scourged and Flayed
Not Loved by your Lover
But Only Played
Walk Away

If you've been not just Used
But Badly Abused
While there's Still a Fire
Running in your Veins
Gather up the White Horse's Reigns

BE NOT AMUSED!
Don't Talk the Talk
Pick up Thy Bed

and
BLOODY WALK!

Let Go

Let go of the People who are not for you
From Congruence not from Pride
If they were not Real from the Get Go
Break the Chains but Love on Inside

Don't Engage with Indifference
And Don't Feel you have to Hide
Save your Love and Energy
For Those Who aren't Obliged

Don't Let Others Steal your Sanity
With their Pompous Crafts or Vanity
Don't Give Away your Precious Time
To Those Who Hate or Socially Climb

Those Who Subtly Ignore or Snub?
Exclude them from your Happy Hub
Fill your Life with Joy and Peace
And Song and Harmony Increase

Protect yourself like a Lioness
From those Who Only Give Duress
From Those Who Sneer or Snide or Flip
Every Time you Let Love Rip

When you Wash them from your Hair
Not Everyone will Meet you There
But It's Not a Popularity Race
Or about Saving your Lovely Face

It's about becoming Whole
It's about Saving your Own Soul
You are Not for Everyone
Realise That? Then you have Won.

Goldfinger? No thanks!!

Don't Bother to Linger
For 007's Goldfinger
Or Pussy Galore
And Her Sex Addiction
Because Ian Fleming
Is Only Fab Fiction

Miss Money Penny
Is Really Uptight
That Naughty James Bond
Won't Ignite her Light!

The Bond Mantra
Is Only Black Tantra
Stay with The Light
Keep your Tantra White
If you're Really Sirius
About Winning this Fight

Being Painted Gold
Won't Raise Kundalini
Even Without
Your Little Bikini
That won't Transform
You Into a Dakini

They Say The Sky is Falling
I Tell You It's Not True
It's Never too Late
For You and Me
When The Truth has
Already Set Us Free.

The Other Worlds

I was Visiting Otherworldly Realms
On an Inhabited Island in the Farthest West
When I saw two Fairies on Moonlit Night
Dancing under an Ash Tree full of Sleeping
Blue Birds

A Storm Whipped up out of Nowhere
And a Man in a Rakish Silk Hat
Muffled Against the Wind
Appeared by my Side
Like some old Jewish Rabbi

He said "Nature always Wins in the End
But we are the Riders on the Storm
And while the Many are Courting and
Marrying
And Gorging on Sugar and Spices and all
Things Nice
They are Unaware that their Fancy Houses
and Palaces
Are About to Blow Away

While you on your Small Island
Away with the Fairies
Surrounded by a Vast Expanse of the Sea
Are Untouched

Relax and Enjoy
For this is Your Time
Pleasure is not Joy
While all that Glisters is not Gold

You will Surf Elegantly through this Storm
With Supreme Confidence
And Ride out the Biggest Waves
Without Breaking your Neck this Time

Nature is Stark and Cruel
But the Realm you Inhabit has Different Rules
And Sweeter Manifestations
And Lightness of Being

The Body is not your Only Reality
The Astral in Flight is Unmeasurable
Yet no Less Real for all That
Time and Gravity no Longer Apply

You have no Need for Embarrassments or
Feeling Small
You are yet Undiscovered though Old in
Years
You are Life Itself Unbounded

With your own Tailor Made Wisdom Practice
You are the Alchemist in your Own
Laboratory
Your Lamp is well Lit in the Holiest of Temples
And in the Morning
All the Little Blue Birds
Sheltering in your Ash Tree
Will Spiral High up into the Azure Blue Sky
On the Breath of a Soft New Wind

You will See a new Heaven and a New Earth
While Still in Body
And the World will be Brand New
Because you Loved
Because you Knew"

****

Knower's Ark

The Animals went in Two by Two
Hurrah Hurrah
The Sheep of Aries and the Goats
Hurrah Hurrah
Chorus;
The Animals went in Two By Two
In The Astrological Zoo
And they All went Into the Ark
Just to get out of the Rain

Verse;
The Animals went in Two By Two
Hurrah Hurrah
A Bull and a Cow for Taurus now
Hurrah Hurrah
Insert Chorus;
The Animals went in Two By Two
Hurrah Hurrah
The Big Bear Ursa Major
And the Little Bear Minor Too

(Insert Chorus;)
The Animals went in Two By Two
Hurrah Hurrah

Two Asses in Cancer Two By Two
Hurrah Hurrah
(Insert Chorus;)
The Animals went in Two by Two
Hurrah Hurrah
Two Lions in Leo Two By Two
Hurrah Hurrah
Insert Chorus;
The Animals went in Two By Two
Hurrah Hurrah
The Scorpions and Eagles Two by Two
Hurrah Hurrah
Insert Chorus;
The Animals went in Two by Two
Hurrah Hurrah
Two Fishes In Pisces Two By Two
Hurrah Hurrah
The Animals went in Two by Two
Hurrah Hurrah
Corvus the Crow and the Lily White Dove
Hurrah Hurrah
The Animals went in Two By Two
You Know it's the Astrological Zoo
It's Time to Understand the Ark
If you want to get out of the Rain

The Pioneer

I see an inventor
A Pioneer
A mad scientist
Performing a laboratory experiment
Pushing the boundaries
Testing the unknown
Finding the answers
You know how
But you also understand why

I see cleverness
A quicksilver mind
And a versatile intellect
But remember to be willing to fail
To learn to become the alchemist

Trust in your as yet undiscovered talents
Never deferring your dreams
Do not indulge a sense of helplessness
Enjoy the spontaneity of mind
The pre requisite of your genius

There is nothing you cannot deal with

I see a large group of people
Outfitting a large canoe
At the start of a journey by water
I see you uprooting as a family
Surrendering to the will of the collective need
For joint concerted action
Under dynamic leadership

I see methodical effectiveness
Others lending a hand
In your role as a leader

I see technological skills
Overcoming nature with machines
Gaining power with this knowledge
Survival instincts kicking in
Compelling coping mechanisms

I see a hydrometer
And I see your mental capacity for machinery
Which must not lead you
To deny what is entirely of the earth
Nonetheless being necessary to our joint
evolution

Whatever occurs you end up better off
You turn everything to your advantage
You capitalise on difficulties
You shape events to suit your own
convenience
You know that worrying over trifles is entirely
self defeating
As you measure physical realities efficiently

I see two Prim Spinsters
Turning within
As two maiden aunts living together
Sitting in dignified solitude
Bizarre maybe, farcical even, and little sad
Superficial relationships
Waste your precious energy
Poise and serenity develop
When you spend time in peaceful solitude
You learn Being and not just Doing
Others are draining
Even dangerously so
At times retreat is appropriate

The soul suffers a loss of uniqueness
You can turn your back
On worthless relationships
Which are spiritually unprofitable
Rejecting their lesser rewards
Mindless pretence of virtue
And distinction
Are poor substitute
For the true unfolding of your inner qualities

Insulate yourself from corrosive influences
Live with access to your soul's spiritual
wisdom
Do not be caught up in vanities
Which preclude real accomplishment in life

Reflect wryly on the day's conversations
Understand the shallow
And the workaday mode of existence
Your life experience is impoverished
By those who exalt in such

Great pleasure can be found
In isolation far from the madding crowd

I see a quiver filled with arrows
The fight for survival triggers aggressiveness
Whether you choose to conquer
Nature, weaker individuals
Or your own base instincts
Is a prime indicator of your spiritual station

You do not spend your arrows for fun
You do not wish to carry them
Skills are your weapons
Creating abundance
You have a right to exist free from attack
Permissions and moral rectitude are
By no means always sufficient

Preparation, practice, power
Are your motto
Be not seduced, deceived
Overpowered or effectively enslaved
Be empowered by your appetites
And abilities to take what is yours
And do it with a clear conscience

.

I see a daughter of the American revolution
Should you be more revolutionary or more
conservative?
One seeks change
The other glorifies the past
To be rebellious or to be more youthful?
Discontented and restless
The tendency with age
Is to maintain the status quo

Good leaders gently guide
Individuality arises within a setting
Of Parental and cultural influences
Life is more evolutionary than revolutionary
You conform to inherited standards
Of behaviour and belief

Your willingness to fit into a group
And its patterns of thought and activity
Generates feelings of stability
Dependability, warmth and trust

You need them,
Enough to limit the degree of your absolute self-
expression
So that your presence in the group is felt as
empathic
This phenomenon of rapport allows for enduring
relationships to occur
In the formation of a heart-connected network

Of course, there is with this a real danger of
stagnation
And acceptance of the lowest common
denominator
So you must not resist change
However conservative we may be
Life is change and the absence of change is
death
Peoples and people die off
Unless changes are embraced

In order to act together as a unit
A group needs to be led
And thus we see that the act of unification
Necessarily throws up the need for leadership
The leader is better seen as a result of the
group process
Rather than the cause.
The purpose of the role is to infect the group
With the inspiration to move

I see a Royal Coat of Arms
Enriched with precious stones
A responsibility of High Office
A noble lineage
An elevated soul
Aristocratic in the political sense
Kings were once genuine spiritual leaders
You resonate at the aristocratic
Level of soul consciousness

You have impressive ancestry
And a coat of arms
You assert authority
And claim your prerogative
Of special importance
The establishment of royalty
Brings great dignity
To the experience of life
You are no accident of birth

The elite group of stewards
Will have the duty and the gift
To bring together
All in common purpose
And unified stability
This projects a future
Of betterment
A vision of hope
And prosperity for all

Do You See Me?

I Will Test you Now
Upon your Quest
Aspirant Knight
Of the Bright Realm.

Are you at the Helm?
As the World is Burning
And the Age is Turning?

Do you See Now?
Do you See?

Do you See Yourself?
Do you See Me?

Did you Dig Down Deep
To Find the Gold Within?
Are you Now in Bliss
When Breathing Out or In?

Will you Happily Cross
The Deepest Ocean Wide?
Will you Stay Without?
Or will you Come Inside?

Can you Divine E-Motion?
Will You Brave the Fire?
In City or in Forest
Can you Quell Desire?

Have you Filled your Cup?
Can you Read the Stars?
Have you yet Truly Unified
Your Venus and your Mars?

Can you Raise the Sun
Right Above your Head?
Can you Walk the Ether?
Are you Rising from the Dead?

Is your Body Armoured
Or are you Dancing Free?
Did you Find the Answers
And the Holy Key?

Who AM I?
Who Are You?
Do you Know Now?
Do you Know?

Do you See Now,
Do You See?

Do You See Yourself?
Do you See Me?

And You? Who are You?

You are Beauty Beyond Thought Conceptions
You are Suffering
And Death on a Self-Made Cross
You are the Peace in a Breath
And the Sorrow in a Sigh
You are the Hope of the World
And Love in a Cry
You are Mercy's Kiss
You are Untrammelled Bliss
And Yet you are None of These
You are not the Pain
Nor Even the Bliss
You are Nothing
As you Die in your Sleep

And I?

A Woman who has Known Passion and
Sorrow
If my Teeth Rot in my Mouth
With Age
I will Remember Love's Kiss
And be Sustained

Before I Die

Before I Die
I want to learn how to Live
And Dying while Living is all I can Give
I'll Pay the Piper and Call the Tune
And Disappear while Dancing
Under the Moon

A Pina Colada

I see you in a crowd on a beach
Sipping a Pina Colada

You are hot
You are wet
You are hungry
There is sand in your hair
And between your toes
Everyone on this beach is your friend
Life is free and easy
When you bring yourself to the table

You move along ignoring the coarse and the
too loud

I see you as a Greek Muse
Weighing new born twins in golden scales
You balance the rational
But must optimise your opportunities with the
non-rational
The left must balance the right
For wisdom to reach its height

Everything is this or that
You live your life making choices between
opposites
Whether you choose with mind, body, heart or
soul
Determines who you become

We are born to fail and to risk failure
The muse is accessible if and when you tune
in

I see children playing around five mounds of
sand
You are one of a very small number of people
Who have awakened to a higher level of
consciousness
Yet your inner child is as yet undeveloped
Humanity is on the brink of a new phase
And your creativity will be required

Being true to yourself is paramount
A child has no need to be reminded of this
Social niceties are such bore
In a world beset by ambition and fear
The light hearted and trusting are rare

Strangely relaxation gains influence
Life can be lived in innocence
If we so choose
The best in you still lies dormant
And will awaken spontaneously
When the time is right

Your need is for profound purpose
Not of inept responses to what occurs
Nor stilted conversations born of superiority
complexes

The Loving protection of Capella
Is your wisdom
As Above So Below

I see a woman drawing away two dark
curtains
Closing the entrance to a sacred pathway
The veils are drawn aside
Life speeds up
The fun starts
Adventure is matched by courage and
curiosity
The twin veils are ignorance and fear

Here is the answer to all your questions

You have the spirit of daring
You must risk foolishness
To reach out to beyond
That which is safe and assured

In you is the spirit of the depths
The path to inner wisdom
The path to the self
The road less travelled
Entrance only for the tried and the true
The rabbit hole guide to the underworld
The Rite of Passage
The mystery school
The spirit of the depths

I see a clown caricaturing well known
personalities
Employing the subtle art of laughter
Diminishing self importance
Ridicule and satire are your comfort zone
You prick overblown authority
But must not lose yourself in the false
authority of those
Who are out to rob your freedom of thought

Life is a continuing self rehearsal
You try to conceal self doubt
Frequently using misguided humour
Making yourself ridiculous

Do not shape yourself
So that others are spared the inconvenience
Of having to adjust to who you really are
Do not go for the cheap laugh
Or you will pay a price
Self exploitation will cost you if you do

You wear a clown mask not to entertain
But because you do not know who you are
You fear being rejected willy nilly
So you try out your mask only with supportive
friends
Who will never know you

The risk of embarrassment started in infancy
Life is trial and error
It is wise to take off the mask when you are
ready
You need not prostitute yourself in caricature
Or grimaces
You are enough
To gain all the attention you need and desire

I see an old bridge in constant use over a
beautiful stream
Making useful things beautiful is an art
Old things, old ways and old ideas
Can be nothing more than outworn evidence
Of a total lack of initiative,
Or an inner lack of vitality or courage.
Old isn't necessarily good
But the chipped, moss-clad, discoloured
bridge
Does not diminish, but enhances the scene

What falls away
As ephemeral as dust upon the wind
Is what does not serve and take its place
usefully
Into this universal pattern of cosmic alignment

Beyond all concerns of fame and fortune
You as the mystic seek to know the ultimate
secret
But you have yet to become the fire
worshipper
Meditating on Ultimate realities
Life is nothing more than a mirror
The world of delusion is convincing
It takes more than gentle heart
and a clear mind to break through the veil

Can you do it?
Will you do it?

It also takes a passionate will.

The divine spark is there every day
To be used daily
Thereby a mystery is revealed
Your state of being can become detached
from externals
You must relax into having no ambitions
Success lies in an end to all wants

Then you can create miracles

I see a large camel crossing a vast and
forbidding desert
As you learn to rely upon yourself
And reduce dependency on others
Who curb and require you to be inauthentic
Or a muted version of yourself
Thwarting your spiritual aspirations
You must minimise what you require of
worldly comforts

You are plodding
Uncomplaining
Uncompromising
And persistent
And you accomplish at no matter what cost to
yourself
A camel is not beautiful
Or elegant
Or famed for its social skills
But like you he knows how to endure

You have good teeth
You are like a dentist at work;
Dentists were invented to overcome the fact
That we self abuse
With sugar, salt and fat
And all Life is destruction and repair

You are required to make known to the world
Your best sacred vision
And to look after your teeth

Better of course to avoid damage in the first
place
Or teeth fall out
Maybe you are a poet?
Or more of a dentist?
All is service

I see you as a girl of five taking your first
dancing lesson
Although not destined to become a prima
ballerina
You may yet put aside your ego to sit at the
feet of a master
As a master is a requirement for self-
optimisation
And you may yet dance within
Higher States are available than those you
have yet imagined

Monopoly

Can I play Monopoly this Christmas?
I hate Monopoly but it's a case of my human
rights
I actually WANT to play Monopoly this
Christmas
I don't even have a Monopoly board;
It went with everything else that went when I
left the ashes of my past life
But I want to Pass Go
And I want to collect £200
Or actually much more than that due to
inflation
I want to take Mayfair off the greedy pigs
I even want to play ghastly charades
I hate charades even more than I hate
Monopoly but I WANT to play charades!!!
With other human beings and not just my pot
plant!
If I do play do I have to disinfect the pieces?
Can I kiss my auntie?
On Christmas Day but not on Christmas Eve?
On the cheek? Outdoors? Holding my breath?

Can I give her a mince pie
If I wash my hands?
But not on a Tuesday to Sunday?
It might be her last Christmas
It might be MY last Christmas
It might be YOUR last Christmas
It could even be all of our last Christmas
But I want to have it
I want to sing carols
I want to go to midnight mass and I don't even
LIKE midnight mass
I want to pretend that most of 2020 did not
happen
I want to wake up and discover that most
humans are really great
In fact I am sure they are
I want to laugh for no reason at all
I want to take my magic wand and make it all
go away

In fact I will
There it goes

Can you feel the extraordinary Lightness of
Being?

I can feel it

Going
Going
Going

Pooooffff

GONE

Birth Pangs of the New Age

Death Throes
Birth Pangs
Jabberwocky Things
With Fangs
Nine Headed
Hydra Snakes
Cutting Off
The Heads of Fakes
Mitigating
Cauterising
Controversial
Nobel Prizing
No More Time
For Rehearsals
Making Sudden
Slick Reversals
Collapsing
Card Packs
Exposing Mean
Virtual Hacks

Time Lines
Con-verging
New Lovers
E-Merging
Precision
Precession
Aforethought Malice?
Holy Chalice?
Changing Guards
At the Palace?
Christopher Robin
Down with Alice
Downloading
Uploads
Uploading
Downloads
Revelations
Thick and Fast
How Much Longer
Will It Last?

A Spiral Universe

Octave after Octave
Division by Precision
Twice Four is Eight
But that will be Too Late
If you Only Ever Wait
For Horrid Polly Ticking
To Put her Kettle On

The Octopussy
Grabs You
With His Oxy Moron

BUT
Boron Is Rare
Made Sparingly
By Spiral Formation
And Cosmic Ray
Spallation

Who Cares for
Billionaires
Of Weaponized
Philanthropy?

When You're
A Zillionaire
Formed By Your
Hearts Past Entropy?

Half a Loaf?
Better than No Bread?

Half a Life?
Better than No Life?

Not for You.
Not for Me.

The Heart is Whole
When Beyond
Philosophizing
And Boring
Procrastination
It's Increased Vibration
Is the Healing
Of the Nation
And your Higher Heart's
Elation

Decaying Systems
Die Hard

But Die they Must
They Form the Dust
From Which You Rise
Under Neolithic
Neon Skies
But can Never Spell
Or Cruelly Meld
A Rubber Soul
In Me or You

The Nine Heads
Of The Hydra
And Ariadne's Spider
Can't Stop you Now
When Like Taliesin of
The Radiant Brow
You Step Into
The Love of NOW

Dust You Are
Dust You Will Be

AND
There's the Rub
My Dear

BUT

You and I Move Silently
In Ancient Bodies
Made from Stars
And We Are Yet Dancing

STILL

Not Bonded But Free

I want to Grow Old
Disgracefully
I don't want their Gold
I Just want to Be Me

I don't want their Diamonds
They are not my Best Friend
They were Only Ever
A Means to their End

I don't want their Wars
They were never Mine
I don't want their Caviar
Or their Expensive Wine

I don't want their Bondage
Or their Sexy James Bond
Or their Licence to Kill
Or their Kicks for a Thrill

I don't want their Lies
Heaped on More Lies
I don't want their Badly
Polluted Blue Skies

I don't want their Meat
I don't want their Greet
I don't want to Watch
Their Coronation Street

I don't want their Medicine
I don't need their Ad-Vice
Or their Spoonful of Sugar
At their Inflated Price

Don't Try to Trick Me
With that Smiley Fake News
Don't Give me those Blues
Or those Paranoid Views

In Case they Don't Know
I AM Not Lost at Sea
I AM Land Born Alive
Not Bonded But Free

Stop making a Fool of Me

I am everybody's fool
But especially my own
Besmirched by lies
My folly was to trust too much
When I saw sincerity in a narcissist's eyes

On Hitting Rock Bottom
I refused Mother's Little Helpers
I knew my own mind
Well enough
To know that soporific fog
Was anathema to my soul

My attempt to swallow the Sun
As Hanuman did
Was perhaps my greatest folly to date
And my wings were clipped
And severely burnt
As I nosedived back to earth
Landing in a caravan of stale memory

Then rage became my folly
At a world's injustice,
Complacency and indifference
In compassion's clever disguise
Whose lies were accepted
As Gospel truth
By the self-serving generation

Better a happy fool if still
Hanging upside down by the left foot
Witnessing silently, helplessly
The folly of the world

Still better an Immaculate Fool,
A witty fool,
Than a foolish wit
With the bit between its teeth
Cheered on by the herd
With gaiety and foolish pride
Or a whole Bullingdon Club

Of Fools
With bluff and bluster
Peppering a few mythological quotes
Here and there
To mystify the hoi polio
And impress
The educated masses
And the rest of the Oxbridge elite
And to seem superior
In wit and intelligence
To the common man
Whom they pretend to serve

Still, that's all you can expect
From an expensive education
And a life of entitlement

Life only throws up a few good men
The Gandhis and Mandelas
The rest are ten a penny
And much of a muchness
In the end
The whole world has gone mad
It is a field hospital
Where the doctors know less
Than the patients on Ward 12
Where it seems a folly to love

When hurt seems inevitable
And the more you give
The more is taken

Yet it is great folly
To stop hoping, feeling and trying
Although trying is trying in itself

Maya Angelou put it better when she said
Love will take everything you have
Until there is nothing left

And that is the exquisite pain
And beauty of it
Love gives all of itself
Then just as hope is dying
It comes back
In an unexpected unasked-for cascade

The worst folly of all
Is not to take the risk of love
Or to only fall in love
But never rise

Don't Come to my Funeral

By then it will be Too Late
Come and See me NOW
Talk to me NOW
While I Live and Love and Breathe
Touch me with your Song
With your Light
With your Peace
With your Beauty
With your Life
Don't Grieve me when I'm Gone
And PLEASE don't Mouth Platitudes
About How Sad it is
And What a Great Shame it is
That we didn't Spend
More Time together
In Fact PLEASE Don't Spend
Your Time with Me
Gift it NOW Or don't Bother
Coming to my Funeral

For Rachel

You are not wishy washy
You are a velveteen rabbit
In a jewellery shop
Your life
Born of Love
Is the crystallized expression
Of your Essence

You are No Prim Spinster
You are a Guiding Light
Pointing at the Southern Cross

Your motto is all for one and one for all

I see a drowning woman being rescued
Because you are part of something bigger

Surrender the need to be special;
And discover how unique you are

You are not alone
Although you often feel alone
Beneath the sham of the world
And after the storm is your peace

Your life rewards clarity
Your world is brightening
In the midst of the deepest gloom
The angels come unnoticed

You know how to create
You put your immortal stamp on the world
By pride at your efforts
By trimming a tree or
Painting a picture
Using your tools
You must learn to contain your wildness
As you generate ever wilder imaginings

I see a hunter shooting wild ducks
Your animal nature cannot be tamed
Nor can it be easily ditched
Denied passions
Do not stay long hidden
What you want you want
And that is it and all about it

Demanding freedom
And lacking inhibition
Make you unusual

Where most would succumb to hysteria you
Understand risk and Cupid's Arrow
You know that all will be well so you
Are fearless and indestructible

You are safe

Base passions find higher expression
In your creativity
Bunnies metamorphose into nature spirits
Yet you are no fluffy fairy
And you know the Ether well

Your soul speaks through poetry
Not prose
You make the ordinary special
In a dynamic way

I see an activist revolutionary
And the force of entropy
You shake the order of things
As you emerge from Chaos

You are a firebrand for justice
A Rebel with a cause
A Ringleader

The rallying cry of your soul
Is to make this world a better place
Not a ranting and a raging falling only on deaf
ears

In her baby a mother sees her deep longing
For a Son Answered
Moulded in your Aspiration

I see a girl's face, yours, breaking into a smile
Acquiescence is not self-betrayal
When it reveals wisdom and promotes
harmony
But the power of it is constant temptation
So Guard against indiscriminate attractions to
pleasure

Your smile is your gift
For it turns your enemy into your friend

I see two men being arrested
Society must impose limits somewhere
Somewhere, somewhen we pay for it all
The carrot is the calmness,
The stick is the price we must pay
If we do not conform to necessary constraints

I see a sunrise at Easter
On Glastonbury Tor
And true fellowship
Mind your thoughts
For they will grow Empires
Which you will live in

Toys and Tinsel

This Christ-Mass
Toys and Tinsel
Are Not Essential
Apparently
Or Even Desirable
BUT
Glitter and Glister
Were Never Gold
And if the True Christ Story
Can Now be Told
You'll be Glad to Throw Out
The Old Year's Lies
Along with Mr Kipling's
Too Sugary Mince Pies
The Essential Oil
Now in your Lamp
Lights the Darkness
Behind Your Eyes
The Revelations
While Still Shocking
Beat Old Santa's
Christmas Stocking

Listen to the Trees

Can you not hear the trees?
They are singing to YOU,
Their healing melodies,
But we chop them down,
And grow palm oil instead.

The flowers so want you
To be well and whole
But we wrap them in plastic
Then throw them away.

We have been taught to call
The Healers Witches
And to Imagine them
With Disneyesque Green Faces
And Black Pointy Hats,
But they are Really
Medicine Women
Like your Grandmothers
Who seek only to Help
And Not to Harm.

They did not Kill,
They were Killed
By the Ignorant and Cruel

The same who now sell you
Back your Birthright
With their Tinkered about
Pills and Potions
And Patents
And Belief "Systems".

Don't Sell yourself
For a Mess of Pottage
Go out and talk to the Trees.
First they will Whisper,
Then they will Shout
And Dance for Joy
In the Autumn Breeze
That you are Awakening
To Truth and Peace
And Divine Healing.

Find YOUR Inner Shaman
And Listen well
To Nature's Symphony
For She is God without You,
Just as You have God within

A Chinese Laundry

I see three baby birds nesting in the top of an
Ash Tree
I see the beginnings of spiritual integration
I see a dynamic balance and harmony of left
and right brain
And an integrated approach

The world is a dangerous place
But I see sanctuary
And protection through elevation of spirit
You risk ridicule and exposure
And falling from the high vantage point
But you are birthing your truth in extreme
difficulty but in safety

You are awaiting your time
You have super 2020 vision
You are able to distance from emotionality
And have flexibility of mind

Your genius is brought into being by this
process
You are a visionary

And you are also practical
You are not the Blind leading the Blind
But the Seer leading the Sleepwalkers

You have committed yourself and your
resources to this end
You can review your actions
Free of worldly concerns

You have the mind of a master chess player
You witness your own thoughts and their
potential consequences
With consummate skill
Before you give them validation

I see a Chinese Laundry
And loyalty to your own way of being
Some parts of how you are
Are who you are
Your integrity depends on sticking firmly to
your principles
You must not capitulate
But remain strong in faith

You are poised, aware and self-possessed
People disdain your work and your worth
Your service has been hidden
But of real and actual importance

Your goals are important
Your occupation unusual
Out of your work comes a betterment for
humanity
Guard carefully your inner state
Make a daily practice of inwardness
And a great richness of life ensues eventually

The incentives seem remote
You endure, unrewarded and even
disrespected
Society rewards those whose achievements
are seen
Not those that are unseen
The culture is immature in this regard

You develop association with the unseen and
the angelic
Which you radiate
You develop exemplary poise

Needing to maintain dignity
Which becomes mastery in practice
Even in irksome situations

Your occupation is specialist
You reach the highest states of inspiration and
creativity
Seclusion at work
Resulting from an unsupportive social
environment
Is in fact a path towards
An unusual depth of inner awareness and
self-possession

I see a tiny little girl
Bending over a fishpond
Trying to catch a fish
You simply ask questions
Powerfully and correctly
At the right moment
With innocent spontaneity
You ask life a question
It answers
You place no conditions upon the given
answer

You engage with reality not with outcomes
Tuning into the beauty of the soul
Every eventuality is exciting
You find something in every situation of value
Hence making everything significant
Unsullied by self-doubt and social conformity

You are able to take the reins of any situation
With a light touch
Riding the white horse
And not the black horse of Intellect
Or the red horse of Emotion
You see what is there
Not what is expected or required
Your perceptions are real
And your influence effective

You are able to self-express to a high degree
With charismatic grace
The smug and selfish
Are rebuked and rebuffed without you having
to do anything
Except enjoy

Worldly achievement is not well supported
Because you always try out the new
But others respond surprisingly well
You bring enthusiasm to the party
Your soul is ever present
And unimpeachable
As evidence of the divine within you

I see your guests reading in the library of a
luxurious home
You have aristocratic responsibility
Aware of current trends and beliefs
These are shaped at gatherings where the
Great and the Good socialise
To be part of this set one must conform to its
standards of behaviour
And beliefs
Or risk being ostracised

The key is relaxation and repose
Which are a valid strategy in moderation
When balanced with effort
The cycle of struggle and surrender
Are the eternal cycle

Ineptitude can be followed by renewed effort
And greater expansion
I see the luminescence of a new dawn
In the Eastern Sky
Blessed with Light
A peak experience
After cold dark days
I see joy in your heart

Genesis is eternally in the beginning
As a current lasting truth
Life is only ever new
We think tomorrow can always be better
But today is always now and the best of all
And all tomorrows come as today

I see two men placed under arrest
Society dispenses punishments
Forces of disorder must be quelled
Revolution and protest are normal aspects of
community life
Society must control its members
Which causes friction and social challenges
You must defend and expand your personal
interests
There is a forceful denial of legitimate freedom
of expression

You must challenge the given order of things
Proclaim your values
And walk your talk
Force is the legitimate tool of the police
When maintaining safety
Society needs to take notice
As more may join in

Rules of society have to be enforced
sometimes
And sometimes protest is legitimate and must
be entered into wisely

I see two Chinese men talking
In their native tongue in a Tower in New York
I see in you the solitude of the spiritual seeker
I see a rapport with them
And a difference with shared cooperation as
the key
And a need to isolate from twin dangers
Which dissolve or crystallise your stance
You have a few like-minded associates
But not in the common herd

You focus your uniqueness
And perfect your life potential
We are all different
But this goes beyond nationality
You meet along the way others who are
similar enough
To understand how to help you refine your
expression

Avoid too many unsuitable associations
And mix with others like yourself

I watch your ideas take concrete form
From your inner vision
You get what you imagine
A normal person's life is suffered
An awakened person's life has a clear sense
that we create the outer
Even to the last detail
It is your mind that creates
A strong mind can interpret the signals of the
soul
And resist the distractions of the body
Holding focus on the goal

I see you as man abundantly crystallised

I see children on a swing hanging on an
ancient Oak Tree
I see your childlike joy at discovery
The exuberance of life
When deep mysteries are revealed
These are the times of the Revelations
A release of emotional excitement occurs
Naive and even childlike
Your soul is free and innocent
As discoveries emerge

Life is delightful
When we give from the heart
You have no fear of danger or authority
You find immediate happiness
Carefree, you maintain zest and vigour
You can now refuse to do what you do not feel
is satisfying
You do only what you love
We are connected in the great web of life
Through higher frequencies of sound and light

Chapter Two; Musings

In the Bardos

Is it like This? You don't have to Answer if you
are too Busy. You surely have other Fish to
Fry NOW!

Only Yesterday you Took your Last Gasp of
this Very Particular Earthly Existence,
Unattached now to Aching Bones or Wrinkled
Skin,
Into a Place where Tomorrow has not yet
Come
And Yesterday is all but already Forgotten.

All Thought and Sense Departed with that
Cloak of Human Flesh that you Wore so Well.

That Light stayed with you.

You KNEW it would!
Knew it well.
I Knew it too, that Light in You.
It is my Hope and my Consolation.

That pure Consciousness which Drives and Lifts and Guides you is Fired up by the Cup you Drank from Each Day, and not the one of Lethe that would send you Tumbling back down into Gross Sense and Pointless Wanderings.

I AM is with you Always, as was said Before, although who really said it seems a little Uncertain Now.

It doesn't Matter. They were Right, and you are Soaring now in Flights of Joy and not Mere Fancy.

Enjoy the Revue my Dear. It must be Quite a Fascinating Saga. The Angels will be Laughing until they Hold their Sides! Your Myth is now Set in Stone here, but Still to be Fashioned Anew for You. Now that I Really would like to See…. but you must Go and Live it First!

Go now. Go Quickly before you Break any More Hearts or have yours Broken Again. You and I both Know that is not Really the Way to Be. Enough have been Broken now.

They had to be. It is Finished.

If you take another Breath, and Incarnate, then maybe it will be as a Bouncing Baby Girl? I Wish you could Tell me…but maybe that is Beyond the Remit?

Wherever you Go Stay with The Love. It is Real.

Chiron
The Wounded
Healer

You Are the House of God

Did you know that you are the House of God?

They didn't tell you that in School or Church, did they?

That Truth went against their System; that was and IS The Problem. It is the Truth that no-one dares to name,
Coupled up with Incest and all other kinds of Mad Secrecy,
Bats in the Belfry and Cobwebs in the Attic.

Only You are the Attic, and the Cobwebs are your Thoughts and Stuck Unevolved E-motions. The Ones they Encouraged and put there and called it Education.

How could they do that to God?

They built Him Enormous Edifices and Cathedrals,
With Coloured Glass and Statues and Altars to their Egos, To Hide from You the fact that the Altar is in You, That You are Indeed the House of God.

They did not tell you that have to Enter it Alone, in Private and meet your Bridegroom in Silence, in your Own Holy Temple, which is YOU, because they did not Know!

It had to be kept from you at all Costs this Truth of course, Or you might have become Unruly, Unbiddable, Uncontrollable. I was all of those and more, I guess. My Poor Mother! No wonder she found me a Difficult Child.

I wouldn't Buckle Down, Knuckle Down or even Suckle Down.

The Rebellion was Painful and Lonely, but Entirely Necessary. I could not be part of their Herd. I preferred to sit out School Assembly, arriving late and sitting with the only other Girl in the School who did not fit their Brief. She was allowed to sit it out and I used to Slink in and Join her in the Upper Gallery of the Assembly Hall.

She was an Indian Immigrant, and her Religion was of a Different Stripe although that was never mentioned. The other Girls who Stood out like Sore Thumbs were the only Black Girl in the School, and the one with the Terrible Acne. We were among the Outcasts, although there were others too, waving their Sick Notes every week because they could not Face the Shared Showers after Gym, or the Endless Boredom of Double Fake History followed by Double Deliberately Complicated Maths, or the School Dinner Queue where the Subjects for Discussion were Boys, Make Up, Boys, the Bay City Rollers, Make Up........I was of the often Silent Horsey Variety, and Eclectic Music Type, but we were a Minority and those Subjects were not Up for Discussion.

It was Torture of a Sadistic Kind to the Sensitive Soul.

School Dinners were Sloppy, cheap Meatballs and Gross Gravy, followed by Spotted Dick or Chocolate Pudding with Lumpy Custard, and we were Young and Hungry and stuffed down the Slop with what seemed to approximate Gratitude.

Vegetarianism was not on the Menu. It did not fit the Brief. Politically Incorrect of course! Indeed I was told if I did not eat my Meat I would Die! Fear Mongering! What a Lie! .....But they had Swallowed It, and so therefore must we!

Still, YOU ARE THE HOUSE OF GOD. That never changes. It is just that we have Allowed the Money Changers in. You can Throw them out. That is the Good News. Do it Today!

I don't Hear anyone Shouting it from the Rooftops?

Some Prefer to Go Quietly Insane

Belief Versus Knowledge

These days it makes me laugh when someone says they don't agree with what I believe because I don't believe anything. I know what I know and I certainly don't wish to force anyone else to know it! If they want to, they can learn about things I know for themselves; if they don't want to then fine, I have no problem with that. If they do want to then I can share but I have no investment in that. I am not interested in making anyone believe anything. Just don't judge me for something you are projecting on me. If you believe that I believe something and I do not, that is projecting. It is ignorant and it is arrogant. I, for my part, do not judge anyone for not knowing something. I might feel sadness, pity even, but not judgement. That is not my business.

Belief has been our problem for thousands of years. We are now in an age of Knowing. I don't mean Scientific Knowing because the danger is that Science will become the new Religion and it is also theoretical and not about true knowledge.

All science only holds until another theory falsifies it. All science is falsifiable. My point here is not that we can't or should not use scientific theory; we have to when it is all that we have. Of course sometimes a scientific theory wins out only because of MONEY and not because it is the best theory. Science changes constantly. We believe things, sometimes for thousands of years, until they are falsified, or we wake up to the truth. Then many are so arrogant that they act as if they knew all along. Many take things we know now for granted and without gratitude to those who brought about the actual knowledge. Many call things progress when they are actually retrogressive. More arrogance and ignorance!

The kind of Knowing I refer to is the kind that takes you within to your divine connection. That is something you can only ever prove to yourself. When you have then you are satisfied. Only you. KNOWLEDGE. A small word. An overlooked word. A BEAUTIFUL WORD.

For God's and Goodness sake Look Up!

One of the greatest sadnesses I have in my life, for myself and for humanity, is that we were not ALL taught from a young age to look up at the stars and understand ourselves and the workings of the universe. Not taught our place in it.

In fact we were told not to look up or study the movements and meanings of the stars and planets. That is why most people still do not do it. The fear of eternal punishment was the threat that was used to stop us.
We are still being controlled by that fear, and now by a whole new raft of fears.
Fear is anathema to life, and to LOVE.
We were told, even in the bible, that the stars were to be as Signs, yet astrology is still seen as profane by the masses. They will pay a great price for this ignorance, along with forcing everyone else who has actually bothered to rectify this lack of understanding, to pay the price along with them.

It is impossible to underestimate how damaging that one single thing has been to humanity, and how much damage was and is still done to other humans and the planet because of it.

In fact it is FUNDAMENTAL to understanding how we are controlled, how we have been controlled, and how we WILL be controlled if we do not address it.

It is the universal language and the Law of God. Astrotheology. The Holy Science of Light.

Smashing particles together to find God? REALLY???

That is like removing a living person's heart on the pretext that you are looking to see if there is love in it.

Very interesting, of course, that mysterious things exist perhaps, but is all this stuff another distracting sideshow? Who has all this "science" really helped? How many has it harmed? Do we even know? Does anyone actually care much? Who asks the uncomfortable questions? Anyone?
If stuff is labelled science, even when it is obviously suspect, we just say, OK it must be alright because they call it science and fund it with OUR cash. Chuck in a few "mysterious" names, numbers and symbols etc. and everyone can be hoodwinked.

The scientists know no more than we do about this stuff really. They cannot accept that there is MYSTERY. They don't want to appreciate it; they want to take it apart and then put it back together.

It often won't go back together or go back in the box. It blows up in their faces, and then in our own. It makes a mess, all this befuddling nonsense.

Then they want gongs, prestige, "universities" named after them, permanent historical adoration, accolades and shed LOADS of money. A Trophy wife or three is also desired and often forthcoming. Happiness? No!

Is any of this going to make much or any difference to your actual life? Especially now? Let's not knock all science, much of it is very useful even when it could have been done much better without such crazy cash incentives being at the core, but it is all falsifiable, theoretical and cannot offer you God on a Silver Platter, however much they try to tell you that it already has. It has NOT. In fact, many of these scientists have removed God from the equation altogether.

Deliberately. They have made science the new religion and it is far far worse than some of the old ones.

Will they next be announcing that the aliens have arrived just to add to the mayhem? Maybe there will be a special pill that you have to take so that the aliens cannot whisk you away to the war planet? Made by BIG FAAARMURR of course! It is humans that cause war HERE! Some feed on it. Some suffer because of it. Those who think that they will find God by smashing "particles" together at immense speeds and stupefying expense and calling "particles" Higggggs Booooson and such like silly names, need more than their heads examining. Perhaps they should be rounded up and injected with a LOVE injection? ....or stood up against the wall, or put in LOVE camps, and showered with rose petals until they capitulate and start to act like human beings?

When will humans wake up to the fact that God/Goddess is within US? Not out there on some planet, or in a tiny particle that may not even exist. Even if it does exist it won't help people to be more loving, which is why people don't find God.

It is why people keep looking in the wrong place for God; because they have not made the connection that God is within them and not on the outside, whether you go macrocosmic or microcosmic. They are still looking on the outside. It is the wrong place. The kingdom, as we were told, is WITHIN.

The media needs to stop whipping this stuff up. It is an expensive harmful drain and helps no-one.

Let them all go and live on the moon. It will not support them for very long. Let us have our lovely Earth back.

When they drag God into it, it actually p*sses me off!

Maybe the new intergalactic radio signal will wake some of them up. We can only hope.

End of Rant.

The Sun Sets

The word Set in mythology means just that. It is the setting sun. It also became Satan in astrology because it is associated with the dying Sun. It is when the sun seems to disappear. It seems to have been put out, to have died, but is of course descending down to Capricorn, into hell, the winter solstice, to die on the Southern Cross, and be born three days later on "Christmas Day" when the sun starts to move again after three days stationary in the bowels of the earth at the bottom of the chart. It then rises at 26 degrees heading for Aries and the Spring Equinox. Then in Aries, which is Street on our zodiac, it "rises" in the Spring. Resurrection!

You can see this in the Glastonbury Star Temple if you observe the sun climbing the Tor from the observation platform…at an angle of 26 degrees on the winter solstice. That is why Glastonbury is a Temple…or really an Observatory, because YOU are the Temple. That is the real teaching of all true religion.

You can also see key constellations in the myths rising and setting over the Tor. Really it is just about how day turns to night and summer changes to winter in a cycle.

Noah's Ark is really a story about the precession of the equinoxes. It is an ancient story in all cultures, amply demonstrated in our zodiac. That is why it is SO important. Noah means rest. All the bible names have meanings that are significant, and ALLEGORICAL! It says so in there! When you have this understanding then you can rest.

Isn't that beautiful enough for you? You need books and beliefs that cause you to hate and kill??? Surely not!

Simple, Universal and TRUE!

It all comes from the ancient religions, and was adopted as a literal story. It was expunged from history throughout the dark ages. We are only emerging from them now.

The Osiris myth is the most elaborate and influential story in ancient Egyptian mythology. It concerns the murder of the god Osiris, a primeval king of Egypt, and its consequences. Osiris's murderer, his brother Set, usurps his throne. Meanwhile, Osiris's wife Isis restores her husband's body, allowing him to posthumously conceive their son, Horus. The remainder of the story focuses on Horus, the product of the union of Isis and Osiris, who is at first a vulnerable child protected by his mother and then becomes Set's rival for the throne. Their often-violent conflict ends with Horus's triumph, which restores Maat (cosmic and social order) to Egypt after Set's unrighteous reign and completes the process of Osiris's resurrection.

The myth, with its complex symbolism, is integral to ancient Egyptian conceptions of kingship and succession, conflict between order and disorder, and especially death and the afterlife. It also expresses the essential character of each of the four deities at its centre, and many elements of their worship in ancient Egyptian religion were derived from the myth.

The beautiful part is that Isis puts Osiris together again after he has been dismembered into 14 parts by Set/Satan/Saturn/Chronos/Time. That is really what happens when we remember who WE are. We re-member OURSELVES!

Osiris means OPEN EYE. Meditate as instructed!

Ma-at is Fairness, (Ma or Mother) but Da-at, (Da or Dad) is KNOWLEDGE. It is clearly on the Tree of Life. Our very language comes from this understanding. Call no man Father. Remember that one? Let's start using Da again! Notice that cosmic order comes from Ma-at or the Mother and is balanced by Knowledge from the Father. The true balance of the divine masculine and feminine which is within each of us. We were made ADAM, but our true Source is divine.

In the bible it says "Out of Egypt have I called my son." The Egyptian myths are astrological and the Christ is the Chrism that rises up the spine in meditation and anoints the meditator by opening the pineal gland of the brain so that the light can enter, and fill the body with Light. That is why Jesus says "When thine Eye be Single then thy Body will Fill with Light." The bit the church these days don't tell you is that you actually have to do it! Der!

Thought for the Day on Modern Manners.

Manners maketh man AND woman. For Glasto bods (or fringe dwellers and globe trotters in particular) a so-called shaman/woman is no exception to this rule.

If a man/woman only takes from you or uses you, messes you about, or involves you against your stated wishes with others unknown to you or beyond your remit, which ends up costing you a fortune, and then cannot buy you so much as a cup of coffee as a token of thanks or apology, then don't re-engage!

If they wish to stay in your house, have your Key, and do not wish to keep the most basic stated house rules, then be ALARMED. Be Kind but don't be stupid!

Draw your boundaries. If he/she does not reimburse you for his/her own mistakes then he/she is COWARDLY and not SORRY for having inconvenienced you or cost you money. He/she is also either so poor that he has never done a day's real work or he/she is MEAN. Or he/she is spending all his/her money pontificating and globetrotting finding other mugs to fleece en-route. If he/she gives no token of thanks or gratitude for hospitality or for services kindly rendered above the call of duty then he/she is RUDE. He/she is also endemically UNGRATEFUL!

If he/she assumes they know more than you do on any given subject, esoteric or otherwise, without having the manners to give you a hearing then they are PRIDEFUL and ARROGANT as well as RUDE.

If he/she abuses you in private and lies about you in public stay SHTUM. A Liar will always carry on with the lying and they get so good at it (because they have a lot of practice) that everyone will believe them and not you. So don't go there. Usually, a Judas will hang themselves in the end. Just wait.

If a so called shamanic "friend" falls for the lies of such a man or woman it is called the Desdemona complex. There are Iagos everywhere even in the Glasto Bubble of Fairyland and Toytown.

If your friend's loyalties are with such a person Let It BE. Birds of a Feather flock together and that does you a favour in the long run. They may or may not wake up to the Iago, but it is not for you to point out the lies. That only gets you deeper into the mire, which you are rising above. Of course, in the short run it can be painful, when a friend dumps you with divided loyalties that have been deliberately divided by lies, but it does not have to be agonizing if you can detach. The same goes in families, workplaces, anywhere. They are all simply showing you their TRUE COLOURS, which may not be the ones they show to the world. So take heart and don't be hurt by such moronic behaviour. Even from a so called Shaman who plays lovely tunes on a reed pipe or writes syrupy poetry to the goddess.

If he/she says they are SORRY with ifs or buts or only words and no remedial action then they are LYING.

If he/she accepts or turns down an invitation without manners he/she is UNGRACIOUS. You then know he/she is not a shaman/woman! If he/she dumps you in it you also know that he/she is not a GENTLEMAN or GENTLEWOMAN! The same definitely goes for the female type of the species! Just because they spout semi-kool astrology or bang a shamanic drum with a picture of a spirit animal (a bat or some such) they are no exception to this rule! Of course the real kind of Shaman / woman DOES exist, but they are RARE. Like Hens Teeth!

Conclusion. Just let your NO be NO and your YES be YES with MANNERS. It takes less time than being RUDE and it has the sweet plus and aftertaste of KINDNESS....it takes you everywhere you wish to go!

NB. For Glasto dwellers....you don't even have to call yourself a shaman! You are a decent human being PURE and SIMPLE.

Manners are in fact the least you can do. Better still be KIND.

Camelopardalis

I switch on my app, Star Walk 2, on my iPhone and I keep seeing Pegasus, Cassiopaeia and Camelopardalis. They point directly to them in the sky. The Bible is written up there for sure!

Cameleopardalis; The Giraffe in the Sky.

The pole star appears to be next to and behind his neck as well as on the little bear?

I love the guy with the sickle and the shepherd's crook calling in his sheep from the sheepfold, the sickle for Time and Saturn, with the deer with his antlers, not with horns. Has to be Jesus returning with The White Hart....

He is heading for Cassiopaeia, the Bride. He must be the Bridegroom.

Camelopardaiis is meant to be a giraffe! Does not look much like it here. It also has Cam in the name. Camelot?

The little shepherd is standing on his back walking away in the other direction. The Giraffe faces Draco.

Perseus, next to Cassiopaeia is where the Light is streaming from now with the most powerful photons ever recorded. Wow!

Custos Messium…does that mean Messiah? And who is Tarandus? He is the Reindeer. That is why he accompanies Santa! Your personal North Pole! The gifts from the North Pole come from your meditation!

The awakening of the Christos, which is the Chrism that rises up the spine and lights the Pineal. Then you feed on the manna. The Divine Bread. WITHIN YOU!

The name Custos Messium is a punning reference to Charles Messier, the famed comet hunter who created it, and in fact the constellation was often known simply as Messier, particularly in France. Its brightest star was the present-day 50 Cassiopeiae, of 4th magnitude. They got rid of it of course! Too controversial.

....Maybe someone just did not want us to see the Messiah up there!

Put your Bibles down and Look up. This is where it was ALWAYS written! Revelations are made of this!

Miss Rose and the Elf

Miss Rose went for a walk and huddled under her favourite oak tree, with her arms wrapped around her knees and a carpet of golden leaves at her feet.

She wept.

So sad she was that an Elf Elder, who had been watching her from afar for some time, made bold and showed himself.

"Why do you cry Miss Rose?" he said kindly.

"Because my friends are all unhappy, the world is changing too fast, people who are well think they are ill and people who are ill are not getting help and dying. Many are dying. Many have lost their jobs and are likely to lose everything. Everyone is being turned against everyone else, even those who loved each other before. No-one seems to know what is really happening and it is almost too late to stop it all now"

"Well, I can help you out there Miss Rose. If you can understand a little Elvish?

You see the people don't yet understand Elvish because they have had Leeeeegaleeeeze thrown at them for far too long, along with words coming out of boxes and talking heads. Words like the Wuuurld EEEEk-O-NO- Mick For Us But Not For You Ummmmmmm, and thingummys like that.

They have gone a bit Soporifffickied, because they are not used to having Time on their Side. That is because they were told Time is Mooooney, but Time is Really Art from the Heart. Now they don't feel rested they feel scarified. A lot of them don't really want to go back to wuurk either, because it was Onerus. But they will start to understand, but only in the Nick of Time. Before the Thummmby Screweeeey things come out THIS TIME, because they will remember. They remember that almost everyone really has Love in their hearts you see Miss Rose. They will take off the Blindfolds along with thegaggywaggydoodahthingamyjiggs, you see?

They will realize that all of the Mooooney in the Wurrld can't give them their lives back. Any and all of them. Ever.

They have time to read the small print now because they have been locked up and down and all round about too! The Naughty Peeeeeeps did not Bank on that one!
It was always in the Nick in Time that things got put right you see?"

"So what do we do?" said Miss Rose hopefully.

"You don't really Do Anything Miss Rose" said the Wise Elf. "But now you can see you will know how to Proseeeed."

"Who are you" said Miss Rose hopefully.

"I am yOur Self without the S. Without the Snake in the Grass.

You are my SEIf and I am Your ELf.
"Good Day Miss Rose".

The Elf did a little jig, his smile broadened into a happy laugh and he disappeared like a puff of smoke.

Thoughts for the Day............

Love is not Wishy Washy and Peace is not Passive. Love sees the Flaws and Errors in its Beloveds and Loves anyway. It knows that the Imperfections will have to be Ironed out, causing Suffering, but it also knows that it is not its Job to do the Ironing! Love is Perfect. Humans are Imperfect. Even the Loving Ones! Even YOU! Even ME!

Know Thyself!

Love Lights the Way. Love does not Judge the Errant Object of its Love. In fact, there are no Objects with Love. Love Encompasses and Conquers All.

Love is not a Small Thing. Love does not confine itself to Love of the Nearest, Dearest, Richest, Sexiest, most Expedient or most Convenient or Familiar Objects. It cannot be Confined. It does not Give Up on Anyone it has Chosen. It also Realizes with Sadness but not with Antipathy when it has been the Depositary of a False, Fake, or Shallow Love from Another, whether that be from a So-Called Friend, Lover, Mother, Father, Wife,

Husband, Brother, Sister or Betrayer. In fact, it Cuts through Fake like a Hot Knife through Butter. Smiling.

Love keeps going where all else gives up. It does not Judge even when it is under Serious Extreme Threat of False Judgments, in Agony, Poverty, or even in Fear of Total Annihilation. Love Reaches a Point where it no Longer Cares. Not that it no Longer Cares about Love, but it no Longer Cares to Engage with Fake Lovers, or about the Judgments of Others, when, BUT only when, it KNOWS them to be False. It cannot be Hooked. Then it is Free to Really Love. How could Anyone ever call that Wishy Washy?

However, there is a Rider to All that. Love does not wait around for Love to be Returned. Why should it Wait? It is LOVE after all! It does not even Worry any more whether it is Loved. It KNOWS it is LOVED. Even if that is not a Human Love but a Divine Love. That is its Sustenance and is Enough! It knows when Human Love in a Given Situation is Unlikely and even when it is Impossible, yet still it does not Give Up. Not Entirely. It Leaves the Door Ajar if not Wide Open any more. It does not

Give its Keys away. It Protects Itself. It Loves Itself. It may Cease to Engage or Care in the Old Way, but is not Closed to Healing or Sharing Itself.

Love Walks Against the Tide of Humanity. It Flows Uphill. It Ignores Unfair Criticism. It Breaks the Rules. It has its Own Rules. It Can Walk Alone For as Long as it is Asked to.

Peace is not Boring. It is Dynamic. Peace does not Sit Back and Give Up. It works for Peace. It does not Engage with its opposite because it has no Opposite. It Hates No-one. It Judges No-one. It only Loves. Peace is about becoming NOBODY. While the World Drowns in Polarity Politicking, Peace enjoys the Peace. It Spreads the Peace. It Engages Others in the Peace. Why? Because it IS Peace.

If it is Wishy Washy and Passive then it is Neither Love nor Peace. If it is Dynamic and Misguided or Selfish then it is not Love. If it is Weak and Passive then it is not Peace. When Love is Strong and Peace is Dynamic it is PERFECTION.

Astrology and the Importance of Kindness

There will be a big conjunction of Saturn and Pluto in Capricorn this coming January, (2020) but the really big one is on Dec 21 2020 when Jupiter and Saturn conjunct in Aquarius. They are all big hitting planets. Saturn is also Satan/Kronos/Father Time in astrological language, and Jupiter is seen as Jesus/Zeus. The great malefic and the great benefice.

Jupiter is expansive and Saturn constrictive. Pluto completely transforms, in this case in Capricorn and therefore ways of government. Much will be forced to the surface and into the light to be healed. Better to do the inner work and not project outwards onto anyone, including the politicians.

Don't give your inner authority (Saturn) away by projecting it outwards onto others. Take as much responsibility upon yourself as you are able. This is really the beginning of the new Astrological Era and end of Patriarchy.

The rest of it is all the death throes, and they are always painful.

There has been much imbalance in the outer world, and it all comes down in the end to the masculine feminine divide and imbalance and how we personally have dealt with it within ourselves.

A new fairer order will result. Whether you like it or not will depend on your past actions and beliefs. If you have been fair in your attitudes and actions then you will love it. If not, then you will hate it.

Why? Because it will impact your own chart.

Don't judge but do observe. It is observing that makes our own reality anyway as the observer always affects the outcome, even in nuclear physics. Even by doing "nothing" you will affect outcomes.

What you will observe is how others treat you and others, and how they consider themselves. Do they put themselves first or last? Are they acting with or without manners?

Do they smile at strangers or only at old friends? Do they even bother to make new friends?

Can they let go of outmoded and outdated relationships that do not serve? Do they judge or even bother with those not in their group or clique? Do they welcome newcomers or cold shoulder them? Are they ever on time? If not then they are not considering your time to be as valuable as their own.

Do they bother to keep appointments or dinner dates with you? Do they let you down at the last minute with feeble excuses? Do they do what they say they are going to do? Is there an energy exchange of any kind? Is their "no" a "no" and their "yes" a "yes"?

If not, they are stringing you along. Are they happy for you when you do well or do they prefer you to fail? Everyone fails sometimes, it is how we learn. Are they grateful for assistance offered or love rendered or are they acting in an entitled, arrogant, superior or selfish way?

If you are a bit low or unwell, or not looking your best, if you are down or recently widowed are they interested or disinterested? Are they self-seeking or concerned? Are they helpful or have they an agenda? Are they projecting their own faults on you expecting you to mirror them? Are they a bit surprised when you don't, but you just hold up the mirror so that they can see themselves?

Do they accept the reflection or deflect it? Are they just wanting to make money or kudos out of you or others? Do they give as much courtesy to the grieving widow as they would give say to a young sexy girl? Do they buy you so much as a cup of coffee for generosity received? If not, then they have no manners, no heart and no hope themselves that others will treat them well when life hits them with painful circumstances.

If you have a boyfriend/girlfriend, partner or lover are they playing fair with you? Is there a balance of give and take? Are you fulfilled? As much to the point is are they fulfilled? Are you stuck in limbo with them or are you both still growing?

Are you playing the martyr or the victim? Are they? If you are then it might break down to make way for a new kind of relationship. This can either be pleasurable or painful. Up to you.

It matters not whether they belong to the esoteric heavy mob or not, or if they are rich or poor. It all comes down to manners and, more importantly, kindness in the end.

As you give so you receive. It just takes a bit of time sometimes to even out. If someone is rude to you for no reason other than their own ego, then address it and if you get no redress or sincere apology then simply ignore them. The swings and roundabouts will come round to them in the end. It is not your concern. That is called detachment.

I Am Not Going to Heaven without My Dawg!

Who remembers being inspired by the Dog Star and the Twilight Barking from Dodie Smith's One Hundred and One Dalmatians? I read it over and over again with a torch under the covers in bed as a child, and I longed for a dog. I never got one though.

It is the brightest star in our sky.

Sirius is well known as the Dog Star, because it's the chief star in the constellation Canis Major, the Big Dog.

He is Isis's Dog, because the Queen's Chamber of the Great Pyramid of Giza has a shaft that pointed to Sirius in the Sky.

Have you ever heard anyone speak of the dog days of summer? Sirius is behind the sun as seen from Earth in Northern Hemisphere summer. In late summer, it appears in the east before sunrise – near the sun in our sky.

The early stargazers might have imagined the double-whammy of Sirius and the sun caused the hot weather, or dog days.

In ancient Egypt, the name Sirius signified its nature as scorching or sparkling. The star was associated with the Egyptian gods Osiris, Sopdet and other gods. Ancient Egyptians noted that Sirius rose just before the sun each year immediately prior to the annual flooding of the Nile River. Although the floods could bring destruction, they also brought new soil and new life. Osiris was an Egyptian god of life, death, fertility and rebirth of plant life along the Nile. Sopdet – who might have an even closer association with the star Sirius – began as an agricultural deity in Egypt, also closely associated with the Nile. The Egyptian new year was celebrated with a festival known as The Coming of Sopdet.

In India, Sirius is sometimes known as Svana, the dog of Prince Yudhistira. The prince and his four brothers, along with Svana, set out on a long and arduous journey to find the kingdom of heaven.

However, one by one the brothers all abandoned the search until only Yudhistira and his dog, Svana, were left. At long last they came to the gates of heaven. The gatekeeper, Indra, welcomed the prince but denied Svana entrance.

Yudhistira was aghast and told Indra that he could not forsake his good and faithful servant and friend. His brothers, Yudhistira said, had abandoned the journey to heaven to follow their hearts' desires. But Svana, who had given his heart freely, chose to follow none but Yudhistira. The prince said that, without his dog, he would forsake even heaven. This is what Indra had wanted to hear, and then he welcomed both the prince and the dog through the gates of heaven.

The Sirius gateway opens at the beginning of July, and that is when America was founded by the Founding Fathers of the United States of America.

Libera Me

Make No Mistake
Libras Scales
Will Do Justice
At the End of the Age

Glastonbury Life

One of the challenges of living in Glastonbury is loving the weird, the wonderful and even the really annoying people. It is not that hard. The weird and the wonderful are a welcome change from the stuffy, the precious and the self-important, and even the annoying people deserve to be loved.

Harder to distinguish on first acquaintance are the conspiracy theorists and the conspiracy factists. In fact, I have given up trying to work out which are which. It just ends up giving me a headache! Let them work it all out with each other!

241

Man (Woman) Know Thyself. Healer Heal Thyself.

In other words, look within and do not rush off expecting anyone else to fix you. If you are a healer of any kind, you will heal from your wound, out of your wound, and it may not heal.

If you don't heal it, unless you are conscious of it, you will inflict it on others and make bad situations worse. Look to yourself for healing. Love yourself. Don't waste time, energy and shed loads of money paying someone with a piece of paper to tell you what you probably know deep within anyway. That you must dig and find the answers to your own suffering. You must work with it and from it.

Pain is pain. It is inevitable. Suffering is optional.

All that you need has been given, but if you don't look in the right place how can you find what you have always been looking for?

A good healer will tell you that anyway and point you in the right direction. They cannot heal you. They are not a healer if they charge the earth and ask you to come again and again. If they wave smoke and feathers and call it healing. If they love you only as long as you pay them. That is conditional. Real healing is free. The rest is a service that can be a disservice. Real Healing has to come from within you, from forgiveness, from understanding from acceptance and from surrender to the divine. The divine blueprint is perfect.

Let us give up the laying on of hands and baptisms and go on to perfection. Where did it say that? Oh yes, the Bible! It may take a long time coming, a life time perhaps, it may be an instantaneous miracle, but it will come in the end if you persevere. Percival. He pierced the Veil and found the Grail. So can you.

Self-knowledge is ruthless. It has to be. It is also the ultimate kindness to yourself and to others. Even when it does not seem that way to them.

Good News; God is Not Dead.

They were wrong, those University professors who told me God is Dead. Whose insistence was on Marx and Freud and Darwin. Their God may be dead of course. Almost certainly is! Mine isn't. Yours may not be? The End of History they said. Yes, and the beginning of Hers. Mine. Ours. Thank God for that!

What we really need more of though is not History, (which is told by the victors and is a present fiction) or even HerStory or OurStory. What we need is understanding of MyStory. The Mystery! We need Self-Mastery. We need to Understand and Know Ourselves.

That involves not so much Learning as Unlearning. Stripping away Conditioning. Becoming naked before God. That does not necessitate the removal of clothing.

Why is Awakening with a Capital "A" so hard, for men and for women? I can only speak as a woman. I encountered the Glass Ceiling early on of course. Disappointment was followed by a kind of reluctant acceptance. I worked with it. I worked around it. I could not smash it. Still have not.

I traversed it, recoiled without smashing, without worrying too much about the lower incomes and being a second-class citizen within the faceless System. I survived that, just, with the concomitant inevitable judgements that came with it; that I was not as clever as a man, as useful as a man, as important as a man.

That I could not afford decent accommodation and did jobs that were low paid but fulfilled my heart was OK with me. I trusted that all would be well. It was not of course! Trust can be misplaced! It has to be real Trust in the Divine or it is not Trust! I was groping towards an understanding then, but did not really get it.......even when I thought I did. Such is youth. Wasted on the Young!

I was feeling my way. I understood that my quality of life did not matter as much as man's in society, or for that matter as much as a woman's who tried to play their game.

Of course she was doomed to failure; so why beat herself up? I didn't and I don't! My quality of life was amazing because of my inner world, genuine friendships, and experience of the free gifts of Nature; not because I could afford expensive foreign holidays, meals in posh restaurants or Gucci Handbags! I never wanted one of those thankfully!

I did travel quite a bit, at first hitch hiking abroad on a shoe string; living on tossed salads and cottage cheese. The beautiful beaches and sights made up for the lack of luxury. Later on, cheap air travel made it possible to have regular foreign holidays in comparative comfort.

Much harder then, than the Glass Ceiling Brigade are the Stony Heart Brigade of one's Familiars, Religionists, Educators, Medics,

Bullies, Indifferents, Fair Weather "Friends", Partners, Husbands, Boyfriends with Agendas, the Self Interested, the world at large......they come in all guises.....just fill in the gaps. Survive those with a good heart and you really are on your way to Awakening with a Capital "A". Awakening to non-judgement. To Acceptance.

Acceptance is NOT about accepting the unacceptable however. That can never be accepted. Along with Forgiveness it is not a wishy-washy concept. Forgiveness is a sword which frees one from the unacceptable behaviour of others without having to accept it. When forgiveness is not a two-way street it is simply a self-protection device which cuts you free. Like Michael's Sword!

If one is lucky one also has good Husbands, (Wives) Friends and Boyfriends along the way too of course, which does not nullify the overarching theme of this essay. Even if one is lucky, which not everyone is, one still has the terrain to traverse.

The End of all that History of course, must be only a good thing. The end of lies about God, about killings of Tribal peoples, accepted killings of other Religionists and "foreigner's" babies, (which is what war is by the way), the end of eating rubbish food, and watching rubbish TV, the end of harming the innocent animals, and the end of suppression of more than half of Earth's population, can only be a Marvel when it is allowed to happen. Only we can do it. One at a time.

Remember there are no Foreigners. Not really. All of us are foreigners somewhere. Strangers in a strange land. All of us need a helping hand sometimes.

One of the biggest, fattest lies in our History, is that Astrology is only profane and not also sacred, and the pretence that it is not being used at the top of the pyramid. That is one to check out for yourself! We have a Trickle Up system in place, not a Trickle Down as they would have us believe!

In the meantime, one must act as if Heaven on Earth is already here, because it IS. It always was. It was always in our midst if our Inner Eye was open. That is the challenge. Can enough of us open our Inner Eyes before humanity dooms itself? Surely the answer is YES.

There are so many awakened now and understanding the true teachings that we are truly ONE. That you are the Temple and the Church is merely a pile of bricks. So said the greatest teacher we have ever had. In every tradition and religion.

After the interesting talk on Monsegur last night at the Positive Living Group, and hearing once again about the many murders of the "heretic" Cathars, who were Gnostics, along with the murders of just about everyone else the Catholic Church decided God did not like, I realised that the Magdelene energy is really simply Magnetism, which is Feminine, where the Masculine is really Electricity (EL) which will destroy when it is not held in check, or rather balanced, by the Feminine.

We are all made up of both. We all have to individually balance both. That is the challenge, not believing something; knowing it from within. This is why balance between the two, not the war of the sexes which we have seen for centuries, is so important. It is the Divine Marriage when it is practiced.

The Gnostics did not "believe" in Gnosticism or duality, as was portrayed, they practiced Gnosis. It is a daily discipline; hence the word disciple! It is something you do, like eating, sleeping, walking...you MEDITATE!

Then you experience the Inner Light. Once the Decks have been cleared.

You have to give it your time, amidst all the other distractions of life. It is putting God first. The practice is beyond duality. It is the practice of Peace and Direct Knowledge of the Divine. The same knowledge talked about in the Bible, when Jesus says to the pastors of the day " You have taken away the keys of knowledge, you don't enter within yourselves (in meditation, knowledge) and those who are trying to enter, you hinder."

Unfortunately, they are still doing it to this day. It is important to realize that this kind of knowledge is not available in books, not even the scriptures. It is beyond, it cannot really even be talked about..... Each person's experience of it is a personal relationship with the Divine, and therefore unique to that person. It makes us all individuals.

The true masters have ALWAYS taught it on this planet, although it went underground through necessity and persecution. The treasure is within you; that is why the murderers could not find it when they searched the Gnostics! They were Idiots! IGNORE -RANTS!

New Rule for the Naughty Virus

Stay in Bed. All the time.

Do not get up at night to go to the bathroom
as you might trip over your slippers, break
your neck and die.

Don't get up in the day either, in case you are
tempted to leave the house and have a life.
Best to avoid the temptation in case you trip
on the doormat and break both legs.

Don't speak to your friends, family or
neighbours, even on the phone as they may
upset you with their negative attitude to the
new rule.

Don't sing. You might choke on your own
tongue.

Do not eat as you may die of food poisoning,
or slip on the wet kitchen floor as you open
the fridge.

You may drink from the bathroom tap but we
suggest you don't go downstairs to get a glass
of water in your weakened state. You might
fall on a loose bit of stair carpet and lie there
for five days before your rescue dog eats you.

Best not to drink, because you will need the bathroom.

Don't ring the doctor. He will be in bed. So will everyone else.

Don't have sex. Not even a last goodbye "I love only you sh*g". It might upset your dog who will bite you out of jealousy and hunger and you may get septicaemia and die. The dog would then eat you and be very sick. They are not meant to eat human flesh. There would be no-one to take him to the vet. The vet would be in bed too. The neighbours might report you for animal cruelty, but you won't mind as you will be dead.

You won't need to worry about anything. You can just drift off. Don't worry about not being furloughed; you won't need the money. There won't be anything to buy anyway.

You won't need food as you won't be hungry and there won't be much around anyway. The growers, pickers and drivers will all be in bed. You won't even need to learn how to grow food or forage, so that saves you the bother of growing anything or learning about poisonous mushrooms etc.

Keep your phone by your bed so that you can report any neighbours you see walking about outside. When the police come for them stay in bed. The police won't be in bed, obviously. They are there to ensure you stay in bed.

Don't bother getting your car MOT'd. That will save you money. You won't be driving it and you won't be able to get petrol anyway because the oil industry workers will all be in bed.

Most accidents happen in the home, so we suggest you put your bed in the garden. Fewer accidents happen there. Don't mow the lawn. You might electrocute yourself or slip a disc in your back. Maybe take an umbrella but stay in bed.

In fact, if you make a bed like this one no-one will have to come and bury you when you die of starvation/boredom/terror. They won't be able to. They will be in bed.

We will beat this thing.

A very short Astrology Lesson for the Astro Cognoscenti….

Did you Know? Sagitta the Arrow is not in Sagittarius but in Capricorn.

Om is the bow; the self is the Arrow drawn with a thought. As the arrow becomes one with the target you become one with God.

Capricorn decans are - Sagitta, Aquila the Eagle, and Delphinus the Dolphin.

Also, to the Ethiopians, 2012 is actually happening in 2020 because of calendar discrepancies. So all the major predictions for the End Times of 2012 may in fact occur in 2020. It does not mean the End of the World…..but the End of the World as We Know It.

Phew!

About the Author

Rosie Temple was born on the Foot of the Bull of the Kingston Zodiac.

She developed an interest in early life in comparative religion. **On The Tail of the Blue Monkey and The Circus Saboteur** have evolved from her personal journey.

After a serious illness she was left almost housebound for a year and she met a psychic healer who helped her on her long road to recovery and opened up a different realm to her. The Clairvoyant path was not to be without its own pitfalls and surprises, however.

Her illness raised questions about identity, particularly as it robbed her of friends, relationships and independence. The invisibility of her pain aroused little concern or acknowledgement in others, even the medical profession, and her local vicar told her to get up out of bed and get a job when she was unable to even walk. The lack of compassion in one appearing to show the opposite baffled her.

At this stage she was battling with looking for God within and without a religious framework. She also worked as a teacher of English, a tennis and singing coach in North America at a summer camp, and a "houseparent" looking after children and later adults with severe learning disabilities and physical problems. Years of working with such people reinforced a sense of the Divine being within us all, and their simple acceptance of life taught her a great deal.

Rosie is a qualified practitioner of Acupuncture and Chinese Medicine. She practised yoga and studied Natural Healing Methods for a period of five years. She has also made an in-depth study of Western Astrology. Rosie spent years working in large hospitals, and Harley Street, as well as running her own clinics in Windsor, Ascot and Wraysbury, and a Network of Therapists in the mid Thames area. She paints (one of her main interests is the Pre-Raphaelite movement); creates digital art and has a degree in Philosophy and Literature.

Rosie is part of the Pegasus Collective - a voluntary group of artists, musicians and poets who put on free, low cost and charity events to do with the nine muses of Pegasus in the Glastonbury area. She is also one of the Bards of Ynys Witrin, the Glass Isle, Glastonbury.

On the Tail of the Blue Monkey was also an attempt at a literary exposition of the astrological fixed cross of matter. This involves the astrological cross which has the polarities of Scorpio-Taurus and Leo-Aquarius. Through her friendships with people of those signs in particular she explores the way in which she sees them and herself in them through the judgments she has made about them. She is interested in exploring relationships and understanding the astrological implications of them. The book is meant as a testament to those friends. In fact, it was written as a Christmas present to her friends and not intended for publication.

She is interested in sacred sites such as Glastonbury and Stonehenge. She spent some time exploring sites and site names of these sacred sites and how they link in to the imagination and beauty of the inner and outer landscapes.

On the Tail of the Blue Monkey was her first work of what she loosely calls "poems", mystic limericks "they are hardly what I would call High Art!" written as a belated thesis and brings together the different strands of her life and experiences, in a way that she was unable to do as a young woman. It is written as a reply to the questions raised when she was still a young woman hungry for knowledge, but left sinking in the quicksands of concepts, ideas, corrupted politics, illness, confusion and unresolved love affairs. It is her personal response to the Marxist/Freudian bent of her teachers that she has finally been able to voice as well as feel.

Some of the poems are in the universal mind and you have probably heard some of them before, although she actually sat down and wrote them with no direct references.

In memory of Denise Michell.

1952-2020.

Late Lady Mayor of Glastonbury, Lady Druid, Elder Bard, founding member of the Bardic College of Ynys Witrin and wife of the late John Michell.

Printed in Great Britain
by Amazon

84271769R00149